An Invitation to Feminist Ethics

HILDE LINDEMANN

Michigan State University

Boston Burr Ridge, IL Dubuque, IA Madison, WI New York
San Francisco St. Louis Bangkok Bogotá Caracas Kuala Lumpur
Lisbon London Madrid Mexico City Milan Montreal New Delhi
Santiago Seoul Singapore Sydney Taipei Toronto

The McGraw·Hill Companies

 Higher Education

Published by McGraw-Hill, an imprint of The McGraw-Hill Companies, Inc., 1221 Avenue of the Americas, New York, NY 10020.

This book is printed on acid-free paper.

1 2 3 4 5 6 7 8 9 0 DOC/DOC 0 9 8 7 6 5

ISBN 0-07-285023-X

Editor in Chief: Emily Barrosse
Publisher: Lyn Uhl
Sponsoring Editor: Jon-David Hague
Marketing Manager: Zina Craft
Project Manager: Anne Fuzellier
Art Director: Jeanne M. Schreiber
Manuscript Editor: Margaret Moore
Interior and Cover Designer: Violeta Díaz
Photo Researcher: Brian Pecko
Production Supervisor: Tandra Jorgensen

Composition: 10/12 Baskerville by GTS—New Delhi, India Campus
Printing: 45# New Era Matte, R. R. Donnelley & Sons

Cover: *Open Door*, c. 2000 (oil on canvas). William Ireland (Contemporary Artist)/Private Collection/Bridgeman Art Library

Library of Congress Cataloging-in-Publication Data
Lindemann, Hilde.
An invitation to feminist ethics / Hilde Lindemann.
p. cm.
Includes bibliographical references and index.
ISBN 0-07-285023-X (softcover)
1. Feminist ethics. 2. Feminism—Moral and ethical aspects. I. Title.

BJ1395.L56 2005
170'.82—dc22 2005054012

www.mhhe.com

This book is
for Ellen Sudden
in a shaft of sunlight

Contents 

Preface

Three themes in feminist work came together in the late 1970s and early 1980s to give rise to the term 'feminist ethics.' One theme was that of feminist attention to contemporary ethical issues, such as equality of opportunity, war, and rape. Another was that of uncovering sexist biases in the traditional ethical theories. And the third was that of the differences other than gender—such as race, class, sexual orientation, ability, and ethnicity—that can bring different perspectives to bear on ethics. Since then, a rapidly burgeoning literature in feminist ethics has not only enlarged on these three themes but also added a fourth: the development of feminist moral theories.

The majority of textbooks in philosophy contain little of this work, although there are a few exceptions. To be sure, the standard text includes a handful of articles by *women* philosophers, but typically not philosophers—whether women or men—who cite the *feminist* literature and use feminist methodologies. When the work of feminists does find its way into these volumes, it is likely only to be in the form of an essay on childbirth, abortion, or caregiving, as if feminist ethics were essentially about what goes on in the women's hut, away from the rest of the village.

It's hard to say why this is so. In other areas of the humanities, feminist analysis and criticism is reasonably well integrated into the scholarly conversation. Textbooks in literary criticism, for example, include feminist work as a matter of course. The same is true in history, theater studies, religious studies, and a number of areas in the social sciences. For the most part, though, philosophers have only just begun to pay attention to gender, race, and other abusive power systems, as they begin to realize that inattention to these matters distorts philosophical inquiry.

An Invitation to Feminist Ethics is an attempt to encourage further conversation. It's meant to support the efforts of philosophers who may not know much about feminist ethics but want to learn. Its primary audience, however, is undergraduates, both those who have had some exposure to philosophical ethics and those who haven't. It's designed to be small enough so that it can serve as a supplement to the usual introductory textbook, but it can also function as a stand-alone text in courses in feminist ethics, feminist philosophy, women's studies, bioethics, and the like.

The book is divided into two sections. The first section, "Overviews," begins by describing feminist ethics in broad strokes, saying something about what it isn't, as well as explaining what it is. Since feminist ethics is the attempt to understand, criticize, and correct our moral beliefs and practices, using gender as a central category of analysis, Chapter One introduces the concept of gender, as well as drawing contrasts between feminist and nonfeminist ways of doing ethics. In Chapter Two, I provide an overview of the feminist ethicist's toolkit—the set of essential concepts that feminists use to do their work. Crucial among these are the concepts of gender neutrality, androcentrism, difference, and oppression, all of which I put to work on an argument in favor of affirmative action. Chapter Three serves as an overview of how personal identities set up socially normative expectations for how some sorts of people are supposed to behave and how other sorts of people may treat them. Identities are of special concern to feminist ethics, I argue, because they interact with abusive power systems to establish who gets to do what to whom.

Chapter Four is an overview of the impartial, impersonal, universalistic, narrowly rational moral theories that have dominated ethics in English-speaking countries for the last century and more. The overview is followed by feminist criticisms of the approach to morality that is presupposed by those theories. Chapter Five is the final overview chapter—this time an overview of feminist moral theories. Although there are many of these, I confine myself to two sorts of theories: the ethics of care and what might loosely be called an ethics of responsibility.

The second part of the book, "Close-ups," zooms in on three topics of particular concern to feminist ethicists. Chapter Six offers a close-up of feminist bioethics, because bioethics is the most popular ethical discourse—the one that seems to matter to people in all walks of life. It's therefore useful to see what bioethics looks like when done in a feminist manner. Chapter Seven provides a close-up of how feminist ethicists think about violence, because violence, when it's gendered, takes on the guise of harm to women. So the chapter focuses on rape, rape as a weapon of war, and domestic violence. Chapter Eight furnishes a close-up view of ethical issues arising from the globalized economy, because here again gender plays a strong role: Not only does globalization join forces with gender to intensify the oppression of women in debtor nations, but "women's work" has itself become globalized, often with disastrous consequences. The chapter—and the book—closes with a discussion of how cross-cultural moral judgments can be made in a feminist, non-arrogant manner.

Acknowledgments

Many people have helped me write this book. Particular thanks go to Margaret Urban Walker for talking me into the project in the first place and then offering insightful suggestions for improving many of the chapters. Sara Ruddick too has read most of the book in draft and been, as usual, unflagging in her kind help. James Lindemann Nelson completes the troika: Like Margaret and Sally, he gave generously of his advice and affection, and remains my most faithful reader. Jon-David Hague, my editor at McGraw-Hill, has been what every author dreams of, not only because he read each chapter in draft with genuine enthusiasm, but because he became a delightful new friend. Thanks too to the following reviewers, who gave me much good advice, though I didn't always follow it:

Marya Bower, Earlham College
Eve A. Browning, University of Minnesota, Duluth
Susan Castagnetto, Scripps College
Ann E. Cudd, University of Kansas
Lisa Eckenwiler, Old Dominion University

Lori Gruen, Wesleyan University
Bonnie Mann, University of Oregon
Mimi Marinucci, Eastern Washington University
Peg O'Connor, Gustavus Adolphus College

And finally, many thanks to the students in four of my classes, on whom I inflicted draft chapters and whose advice I did follow, as carefully as I could. For all the things I've gotten right in this book, then, I'll happily take the credit. If anything strikes you as wrong, let's just say it's my students' fault.

Part One

OVERVIEWS

CHAPTER

1

What Is Feminist Ethics?

A few years ago, a dentist in Ohio was convicted of having sex with his female patients while they were under anesthesia. I haven't been able to discover whether he had to pay a fine or do jail time, but I do remember that the judge ordered him to take a course in ethics. And I recall thinking how odd that order was. Let's suppose, as the judge apparently did, that the dentist really and truly didn't know it was wrong to have sex with anesthetized patients (this will tax your imagination, but try to suppose it anyway). Can we expect—again, as the judge apparently did—that on completing the ethics course, the dentist would be a better, finer man?

Hardly. If studying ethics could make you good, then the people who have advanced academic degrees in the subject would be paragons of moral uprightness. I can't speak for all of them, of course, but though the ones I know are nice enough, they're no more moral than anyone else. Ethics doesn't improve your character. Its *subject* is morality, but its relationship to morality is that of a scholarly study to the thing being studied. In that respect, the relationship is a little like the relationship between grammar and language.

Let's explore that analogy. People who speak fluent English don't have to stop and think about the correctness of the sentence "He gave it to *her.*" But here's a harder one. Should you say, "He gave it to *her* who must be obeyed?" or "He gave it to *she* who must be obeyed?" To sort this out, it helps to know a little grammar—the systematic, scholarly description of the structure of the language and the rules for speaking and writing in it. According to those rules, the object of the preposition "to" is the entire clause that comes after it, and the subject of that clause is "she." So, even though it sounds peculiar, the correct answer is "He gave it to she who must be obeyed."

In a roughly similar vein, morally competent adults don't have to stop and think about whether it's wrong to have sex with one's anesthetized patients. But if you want to understand whether it's wrong to have large signs in bars telling pregnant women not to drink, or to sort out the conditions under which it's all right to tell a lie, it helps to know a little ethics. The analogy between grammar and ethics isn't exact, of course. For one thing, there's considerably more agreement about what language is than about what morality is. For another, grammarians are concerned only with the structure of language, not with the meaning or usage of particular words. In both cases, however, the same point can be made: You already have to know quite a lot about how to behave—linguistically or morally—before there's much point in studying either grammar or ethics.

1.1. What Is Ethics?

Ethics is the scholarly study of morality. It sets out to *understand* and *justify* people's moral beliefs and the forms of life in which those beliefs are practiced. And it also *criticizes* and *corrects* those beliefs and practices. As an academic discipline, it can be divided into three branches. The first branch is metaethics—the study of what morality is. To engage in metaethics is to ask questions like "What do moral terms mean? Where do moral values come from? Do moral judgments consist of statements that must be either true or false, or are they more like a laugh or an expression of disgust? If moral judgments *are* true or false, are they true just for me? For my society? For everybody? Do we have to do what the moral rules tell us to because they're commanded by God? Because it would be irrational not to? Because, paradoxically, that's the only way we can be free?"

The second branch is normative ethics—the study of moral theories and concepts. The task of normative ethics is to set out and critically examine the *norms*, or standards, that we can use both to guide and to evaluate our actions. Here we find moral theories such as the ethics of care, social contract theory, utilitarianism, Kantian ethics, and virtue ethics.

We also find accounts of integrity, oppression, justice, evil, and so on. You are doing normative ethics when you try to determine what duties you have to your parents or children, or whether you should forgive someone who isn't sorry for having mistreated you. Figuring out the moral difference (if there is one) between making something happen and simply letting it happen is also an exercise in normative ethics.

The third branch of ethics is practical ethics—the study of ethical issues that arise within specific social practices. You will often hear this called "applied" ethics, because on one popular picture of morality, ethics at this level is a matter of taking the principles that you have logically deduced from your moral theory (at the normative level) and applying them to a concrete case. For reasons I'll explain later, this picture of morality seems to me to be mistaken, so rather than talk about applications, I'll describe this branch as the most practical of the three. Examples of practical ethics are legal ethics, medical ethics, the ethics of journalism, and business ethics, all of which set out to regulate the behavior of the people working in those fields. Environmental ethics and bioethics—the study of ethical issues arising from the rapid advances in biomedicine—belong to this branch as well. Here's where you'd work out the moral implications of those signs in bars. And it's here where the debates over abortion, capital punishment, affirmative action, and physician-assisted suicide take place.

For your convenience, I've made a road map of some of the territory that's covered by ethics. It's incomplete, of course, and you probably won't be familiar with all the terms on the map, but don't worry about that for now. You'll pick up the ones you need as we go along.

You'll notice that the word *feminist* appears nowhere on this road map. The reason is that feminist ethics isn't a branch of ethics—it's a way of *doing* ethics. Feminist ethicists work in all three branches. Annette Baier, for example, has written a book called *Moral Prejudices* in which she develops the idea of trust as a moral emotion. That is a book in metaethics, because it argues for a naturalized moral epistemology. In *Justice and the Politics of Difference,* Iris Marion Young explains why social justice requires explicitly acknowledging and attending to the differences among social

Ethics Road Map

METAETHICS

Metaphysical Theories (theories of the basic nature of morality)

Noncognitivism (for example, emotivism): Moral judgments aren't true or false.
Cognitivism: Moral judgments are true or false.
Monism: All moral values are commensurable; there can be no genuine moral dilemmas.
Pluralism: Moral values are plural and therefore can conflict in actual cases.

Moral Epistemologies (theories of moral knowledge)

Foundationalism: Moral truths rest on some fundamental moral claim (for example, the good for humans, the permission principle).
Coherentism: Moral beliefs are true or acceptable if they are consistent with one another.
Moral particularism: What counts as a moral reason in one context may not count as a reason in another.
Skepticism: Moral knowledge may not be possible.
Naturalized moral epistemology: Moral knowledge arises out of and is corrected by our experience of the world.

NORMATIVE ETHICS

Theories	**Accounts of**
Ethics of care	Integrity
Kantian ethics	Oppression
Social contract theory	Justice
Utilitarianism	Evil
Virtue theory	Human good

PRACTICAL ETHICS

Professional ethics (law, medicine, architecture, journalism, etc.)
Business ethics
Environmental ethics
Bioethics

groups that bestow privilege on some and keep others powerless. That is a book in normative ethics, because it gives an account of the concept of justice. In *Environmental Culture: The Ecological Crisis of Reason,* Val Plumwood argues that because those of us who live in postindustrial societies think of ourselves as outside of nature rather than a part of it, we aren't sensitive to ecological limits, dependencies, and interconnections. That is a book in practical ethics, because it concerns a specific moral problem. These authors are all ethicists, and they do what ethicists do. But they do it in a feminist way.

1.2. What Is Feminism?

What, then, is feminism? As a social and political movement with a long, intermittent history, feminism has repeatedly come into public awareness, generated change, and then disappeared again. As an eclectic body of theory, feminism entered colleges and universities in the early 1970s as a part of the women's studies movement, contributing to scholarship in every academic discipline, though probably most heavily in the arts, social sciences, literature, and the humanities in general. Feminist ethics is a part of the body of theory that is being developed primarily in colleges and universities.

Many people in the United States think of feminism as a movement that aims to make women the social equals of men, and this impression has been reinforced by references to feminism and feminists in the newspapers, on television, and in the movies. But bell hooks has pointed out in *Feminist Theory from Margin to Center* (1984, 18–19) that this way of defining feminism raises some serious problems. Which men do women want to be equal to? Women who are socially well off wouldn't get much advantage from being the equals of the men who are poor and lower class, particularly if they aren't white. Hooks's point is that there are no women and men in the abstract. They are poor, black, young, Latino/a, old, gay, able-bodied, upper class, down on their luck, Native American, straight, and all the rest of it. When a woman doesn't think about this, it's probably because she doesn't have to. And that's usually a sign that her own social position is privileged. In fact, privilege often means that there's something uncomfortable going on that others have to pay attention to but you don't. So, when hooks asks which men women want to be equal to, she's reminding us that there's an unconscious presumption of privilege built right in to this sort of demand for equality.

There's a second problem with the equality definition. Even if we could figure out which men are the ones to whom women should be equal, that way of putting it suggests that the point of feminism is somehow to get women to measure up to what (at least some) men already are. Men remain the point of reference; theirs are the lives that women would naturally want. If the first problem with the equality definition is "Equal to *which* men?" the second problem could be put as "Why equal to *any* men?" Reforming a system in which men are the point of reference by allowing women to perform as their equals "forces women to focus on men and address men's conceptions of women rather than creating and developing women's values about themselves," as Sarah Lucia Hoagland puts it in *Lesbian Ethics* (1988, 57). For that reason, Hoagland and some other feminists believe that feminism is first and foremost about women.

But characterizing feminism as about women has its problems too. What, after all, is a woman? In her 1949 book, *The Second Sex,* the French feminist philosopher Simone de Beauvoir famously observed, "One is not born, but becomes a woman. No biological, psychological, or economic fate determines the figure that the human female presents in society: it is civilization as a whole that produces this creature, intermediate between male and eunuch, which is described as feminine" (Beauvoir 1949, 301). Her point is that while plenty of human beings are born female, 'woman' is not a natural fact about them—it's a social invention. According to that invention, which is widespread in "civilization as a whole," man represents the positive, typical human being, while woman represents only the negative, the not-man. She is the Other against whom man defines himself—he is all the things that she is not. And she exists only in relation to him. In a later essay called "One Is Not Born a Woman," the lesbian author and theorist Monique Wittig (1981, 49) adds that because women belong to men sexually as well as in every other way, women are necessarily heterosexual. For that reason, she argued, lesbians aren't women.

But, you are probably thinking, everybody knows what a woman is, and lesbians certainly *are* women. And you're right. These French feminists aren't denying that there's a perfectly ordinary use of the word *woman* by which it means exactly what you think it means. But they're explaining what this comes down to, if you look at it from a particular point of view. Their answer to the question "What is a woman?" is that women are different from men. But they don't mean this as a trite observation. They're saying that 'woman' refers to *nothing but* difference from men, so that apart from men, women aren't anything. 'Man' is the positive term, 'woman' is the negative one, just like 'light' is the positive term and 'dark' is nothing but the absence of light.

A later generation of feminists have agreed with Beauvoir and Wittig that women are different from men, but rather than seeing that difference as simply negative, they put it in positive terms, affirming feminine qualities as a source of personal strength and pride. For example, the philosopher Virginia Held thinks that women's moral experience as mothers, attentively nurturing their children, may serve as a better model for social relations than the contract model that the free market provides. The poet Adrienne Rich celebrated women's passionate nature (as opposed, in stereotype, to the rational nature of men), regarding the emotions as morally valuable rather than as signs of weakness.

But defining feminism as about the positive differences between men and women creates yet another set of problems. In her 1987 *Feminism Unmodified,* the feminist legal theorist Catharine A. MacKinnon points out that this kind of difference, as such, is a symmetrical relationship: If I am different from you, then you are different from me in exactly the same respects and to exactly the same degree. "Men's differences from women are equal to women's differences from men," she writes. "There is an *equality* there. Yet the sexes are not socially equal" (MacKinnon 1987, 37). No amount of attention to the differences between men and women explains why men, as a group, are more socially powerful, valued, advantaged, or free than women. For that, you have to see differences as counting in certain ways, and certain differences being created precisely because they give men *power* over women.

Although feminists disagree about this, my own view is that feminism isn't—at least not directly—about equality, and it isn't about women, and it isn't about difference. It's about power. Specifically, it's about the social pattern, widespread across cultures and history, that distributes power asymmetrically to favor men over women. This asymmetry has been given many names, including the subjugation of women, sexism, male dominance, patriarchy, systemic misogyny, phallocracy, and the oppression of women. A number of feminist theorists simply call it gender, and throughout this book, I will too.

1.3. What Is Gender?

Most people think their gender is a natural fact about them, like their hair and eye color: "Jones is 5 foot 8, has red hair, and is a man." But gender is a *norm,* not a fact. It's a prescription for how people are supposed to act; what they must or must not wear; how they're supposed to sit, walk, or stand; what kind of person they're supposed to marry; what sorts of things they're supposed to be interested in or good at; and what they're entitled to. And because it's an *effective* norm, it creates the differences between men and women in these areas.

Gender doesn't just tell women to behave one way and men another, though. It's a *power* relation, so it tells men that they're entitled to things that women aren't supposed to have, and it tells women that they are supposed to defer to men and serve them. It says, for example, that men are supposed to occupy positions of religious authority and women are supposed to run the church suppers. It says that mothers are supposed to take care of their children but fathers have more important things to do. And it says that the things associated with femininity are supposed to take a back seat to the things that are coded masculine. Think of the many tax dollars allocated to the military as compared with the few tax dollars allocated to the arts. Think about how kindergarten teachers are paid as compared to how stockbrokers are paid. And think about how many presidents of the United States have been women. Gender operates through social institutions (like marriage and the law) and practices (like education and medicine) by disproportionately conferring entitlements and the control of resources on men, while disproportionately assigning women to subordinate positions in the service of men's interests.

To make this power relation seem perfectly natural—like the fact that plants grow up instead of down, or that human beings grow old and die—gender constructs its norms for behavior around what is supposed to be the natural biological distinction between the sexes. According to this distinction, people who have penises and testicles, XY chromosomes, and beards as adults belong to the male sex, while people who have clitorises and ovaries, XX chromosomes, and breasts as adults belong to the female sex, and those are the only sexes there are. Gender, then, is the complicated set of cultural meanings that are constructed around the two sexes. Your sex is either male or female, and your gender—either masculine or feminine—corresponds socially to your sex.

As a matter of fact, though, sex isn't quite so simple. Some people with XY chromosomes don't have penises and never develop beards, because they don't have the receptors that allow them to make use of the male hormones that their testicles produce. Are they male or female? Other people have ambiguous genitals or internal reproductive structures that don't correspond in the usual manner to their external genitalia. How should we classify them? People with Turner's syndrome have XO chromosomes instead of XX. People with Klinefelter's syndrome have three sex chromosomes: XXY. Nature is a good bit looser in its categories than the simple male/female distinction acknowledges. Most human beings can certainly be classified as one sex or the other, but a considerable number of them fall somewhere in between.

The powerful norm of gender doesn't acknowledge the existence of the in-betweens, though. When, for example, have you ever filled out an application for a job or a driver's license or a passport that gave you a choice other than M or F? Instead, by basing its distinction between masculine and feminine on the existence of two and only two sexes, gender makes the inequality of power between men and women appear natural and therefore legitimate.

Gender, then, is about power. But it's not about the power of just one group over another. Gender always interacts with other social markers—such as race, class, level of education, sexual orientation, age, religion, physical and mental health, and ethnicity—to distribute power unevenly among women positioned differently in the various social orders, and it does the same to men. A man's social status, for example, can have a great deal to do with the extent to which he's even perceived as a man. There's a wonderful passage in the English travel writer Frances Trollope's *Domestic Manners of the Americans* (1831), in which she describes the exaggerated delicacy of middle-class young ladies she met in Kentucky and Ohio. They wouldn't dream of sitting in a chair that was still warm from contact with a gentleman's bottom, but thought nothing of getting laced into their corsets in front of a male house slave. The slave, it's clear, didn't count as a man—not in the relevant sense, anyway. Gender is the force that makes it matter whether you are male or female, but it always works hand in glove with all the other things about you that matter at the same time. It's one power relation intertwined with others in a complex social system that distinguishes your betters from your inferiors in all kinds of ways and for all kinds of purposes.

1.4. Power and Morality

If feminism is about gender, and gender is the name for a social system that distributes power unequally between men and women, then you'd expect feminist ethicists to try to *understand, criticize,* and *correct* how gender operates within our moral beliefs and practices. And they do just that. In the first place, they challenge, on moral grounds, the powers men have over women, and they claim for women, again on moral grounds, the powers that gender denies them. As the moral reasons for opposing gender are similar to the moral reasons for opposing power systems based on social markers other than gender, feminist ethicists also offer moral arguments against systems based on class, race, physical or mental ability, sexuality, and age. And because all these systems, including gender, are powerful enough to *conceal* many of the forces that keep them in place, it's often necessary to make the forces visible by explicitly identifying—and condemning—the various ugly ways they allow some people to treat others. This is a central task for feminist ethics.

Feminist ethicists also produce theory about the moral meaning of various kinds of *legitimate* relations of unequal power, including relationships of dependency and vulnerability, relationships of trust, and relationships based on something other than choice. Parent–child relationships, for example, are necessarily unequal and for the most part unchosen. Parents can't help having power over their children, and while they may have chosen to have children, most don't choose to have the particular children they do, nor do children choose their parents. This raises questions about the responsible use of parental power and the nature of involuntary obligations, and these are topics for feminist ethics. Similarly, when you trust someone, that person has power over you. Whom should you trust, for what purposes, and when is trust not warranted? What's involved in being trustworthy, and what must be done to repair breaches of trust? These too are questions for feminist ethics.

Third, feminist ethicists look at the various forms of power that are required for morality to operate properly at all. How do we learn right from wrong in the first place? We usually learn it from our parents, whose power to permit and forbid, praise and punish, is essential to our moral training. For whom or what are we ethically responsible? Often this depends on the kind of power we have over the person or thing in question. If, for instance, someone is particularly vulnerable to harm because of something I've done, I might well have special duties toward that person. Powerful social institutions—medicine, religion, government, and the market, to take just a few examples—typically dictate what is morally required of us and to whom we are morally answerable. Relations of power set the terms for who must answer to whom, who has authority over whom, and who gets excused from certain kinds of accountability to whom. But because so many of these power relations are illegitimate, in that they're instances of gender, racism, or other kinds of bigotry, figuring out which ones are morally justified is a task for feminist ethics.

1.5. Description and Prescription

So far it sounds as if feminist ethics devotes considerable attention to *description*—as if feminist ethicists were like poets or painters who want to show you something about reality that you might otherwise have missed. And indeed, many feminist ethicists emphasize the importance of understanding how social power actually works, rather than concentrating solely on how it ought to work. But why, you might ask, should ethicists worry about how power operates within societies? Isn't it up to sociologists and political scientists to describe how things *are*, while ethicists concentrate on how things *ought* to be?

As the philosopher Margaret Urban Walker has pointed out in *Moral Contexts*, there is a tradition in Western philosophy, going all the way back to Plato, to the effect that morality is something ideal and that ethics, being the study of morality, properly examines only that ideal. According to this tradition, notions of right and wrong as they are found in the world are unreliable and shadowy manifestations of something lying outside of human experience—something to which we ought to aspire but can't hope to reach. Plato's Idea of the Good, in fact, is precisely not of this earth, and only the gods could truly know it. Christian ethics incorporates Platonism into its insistence that earthly existence is fraught with sin and error and that heaven is our real home. Kant too insists that moral judgments transcend the histories and circumstances of people's actual lives, and most moral philosophers of the twentieth century have likewise shown little interest in how people really live and what it's like for them to live that way. "They think," remarks Walker (2001), "that there is little to be learned from what is about what ought to be" (3).

In Chapter Four we'll take a closer look at what goes wrong when ethics is done that way, but let me just point out here that if you don't know how things are, your prescriptions for how things ought to be won't have much practical effect. Imagine trying to sail a ship without knowing anything about the tides or where the hidden rocks and shoals lie. You might have a very fine idea of where you are trying to go, but if you don't know the waters, at best you are likely to go off course, and at worst you'll end up going down with all your shipmates. If, as many feminists have noted, a crucial fact about human selves is that they are always embedded in a vast web of relationships, then the forces at play within those relationships must be understood. It's knowing how people are situated with respect to these forces, what they are going through as they are subjected to them, and what life is like in the face of them, that lets us decide which of the forces are morally justified. Careful description of how things are is a crucial part of feminist methodology, because the power that puts certain groups of people at risk of physical harm, denies them full access to the good things their society has to offer, or treats them as if they were useful only for other people's purposes is often hidden and hard to see. If this power isn't seen, it's likely to remain in place, doing untold amounts of damage to great numbers of people.

All the same, feminist ethics is *normative* as well as descriptive. It's fundamentally about how things ought to be, while description plays the crucial but secondary role of helping us to figure that out. Normative language is the language of "ought" instead of "is," the language of "worth" and "value," "right" and "wrong," "good" and "bad." Feminist ethicists differ on a number of normative issues, but as the philosopher Alison Jaggar (1991) has famously put it, they all share two moral commitments: "that the subordination of women is morally wrong and that the moral experience of women is worthy of respect" (95). The first commitment—that women's interests ought not systematically to be set in the service of men's—can be understood as a moral challenge to power under the guise of gender. The second commitment—that women's experience must be taken seriously—can be understood as a call to acknowledge how that power operates. These twin commitments are the two normative legs on which any feminist ethics stands.

Feminist ethics, then, is both descriptive and prescriptive. The belief that good normative theory requires a solid grasp of actual social practices isn't shared by all feminist ethicists, but it's reflected in enough feminist work to cause what seems to me to be a confusion. Flip back to the ethics road map, and look again at the distinction between normative ethics and practical ethics. In nonfeminist ethics, the division between these two branches of ethics can often be pretty sharp. *Normative ethics* tends to consist of ideal moral theory, with scant or no attention paid to specific social practices, whereas *practical ethics* uses principles extracted from that ideal theory and applies them to something concrete, like business. But when you try to apply the distinction between normative ethics and practical ethics to feminist ethics, you'll find it doesn't work very well, because feminist moral theory tends not to be ideal but instead is grounded in description. And that's what causes the confusion: Many people assume that because feminist ethics is practical, it's opposed to theory, and furthermore, that all feminist ethics is "applied" ethics.

A better way of looking at it, I think, is to see *feminist normative ethics* as moral theory that arises out of actual social practices of all kinds and that in turn relies on those practices to help determine whether it's on the right track, while *feminist practical ethics*—for example, feminist bioethics—offers ethical analyses of specific social practices (like biomedicine). If you think of it that way, you can see that feminists aren't so much opposed to theory as dubious about certain kinds of theory-building and that, even at its most practical, feminist ethics retains its normative bite.

1.6. Morality and Politics

If the idealization of morality goes back over two thousand years in Western thought, a newer tradition, only a couple of centuries old, has split off morality from politics. According to this tradition, which can be traced to Kant and some other Enlightenment philosophers, morality concerns the relations between persons, whereas politics concerns the relations among nation-states, or between a state and its citizens. So, as Iris Marion Young (1990) puts it, ethicists have tended to focus on intentional actions by individual persons, conceiving of moral life as "conscious, deliberate, a rational weighing of alternatives," whereas political philosophers have focused on impersonal governmental systems, studying "laws, policies, the large-scale distribution of social goods, countable quantities like votes and taxes" (149).

For feminists, though, the line between ethics and political theory isn't quite so bright as this tradition makes out. It's not always easy to tell where feminist ethics leaves off and feminist political theory begins. There are two reasons for this. In the first place, while ethics certainly concerns personal behavior, there is a long-standing insistence on the part of feminists that the personal *is* political. In a 1970 essay called "The Personal Is Political," the political activist Carol Hanisch observed that "personal problems are political problems. There are no personal solutions at this time" (204–205). What Hanisch meant is that even the most private areas of everyday life, including such intensely personal areas as sex, can function to maintain abusive power systems like gender. If a heterosexual woman believes, for example, that contraception is primarily her responsibility because she'll have to take care of the baby if she gets pregnant, she is propping up a system that lets men evade responsibility not only for pregnancy, but for their own offspring as well. Conversely, while unjust social arrangements such as gender and race invade every aspect of people's personal lives, "there are no personal solutions," either when Hanisch wrote those words or now, because to shift dominant understandings of how certain groups may be treated, and what other groups are entitled to expect of them, requires concerted political action, not just personal good intentions.

The second reason why it's hard to separate feminist ethics from feminist politics is that feminists typically subject the ethical theory they produce to critical political scrutiny, not only to keep untoward political biases out, but also to make sure that the work accurately reflects their feminist politics. Many nonfeminist ethicists, on the other hand, don't acknowledge that their work reflects their politics, because they don't think it should. Their aim, by and large, has been to develop ideal moral theory that applies to all people, regardless of their social position or experience of life, and to do that objectively, without favoritism, requires them to leave their own personal politics behind. The trouble, though, is that they aren't really leaving their own personal politics behind. They're merely refusing to notice that their politics is inevitably built right in to their theories. (This is an instance of Lindemann's ad hoc rule Number 22: Just because you think you are doing something doesn't mean you're actually doing it.) Feminists, by contrast, are generally skeptical of the idealism nonfeminists favor, and they're equally doubtful that objectivity can be achieved by stripping away what's distinctive about people's experiences or commitments. Believing that it's no wiser to shed one's political allegiances in the service of ethics than it would be to shed one's moral allegiances, feminists prefer to be transparent about their politics as a way of keeping their ethics intellectually honest.

In the following chapters, then, you'll find that power and morality, description and prescription, theory and practice, and ethics and politics all jog along together. I'm not going to try to show you the one way that's most representative of how feminists do ethics, because as you probably realize by now, there's no such thing. Feminists disagree, both with nonfeminists and with one another. But I can show you samplings of feminist moral thought on a number of subjects, so that by the time you reach the end of this book you'll have a pretty decent idea of what feminist ethics is.

In the next chapter I'll give you an overview of the feminist ethicist's toolkit—the set of essential concepts that feminists use to do their work. We've already examined some of these concepts, such as gender, power, and "the personal is political," but you'll need to familiarize yourself with several others before you can start doing feminist ethics for yourself. Crucial among these tools are the concepts of gender neutrality, androcentrism, difference, and oppression, all of which I'll put to work on an argument in favor of affirmative action.

In Chapter Three I'll give you an overview of how personal identities set up socially normative expectations for how some sorts of people are supposed to behave and how other sorts of people may treat them. Gender interacts with other power systems to establish who gets to do what to whom, so feminist ethicists have to pay special attention to how identities function within morality.

Chapter Four is an overview of the impartial, impersonal, universalistic, narrowly rational moral theories that have dominated ethics in English-speaking countries for the past 150 years or so. The overview is followed by feminist criticisms of the approach to morality that's presupposed by those theories.

Chapter Five is the final overview chapter—this time an overview of feminist moral theories. There are many of these, and as you might guess, it's hard to separate them out from feminist social and political theories. So I've confined myself to two sorts of theories: the ethics of care and what might loosely be called an ethics of responsibility.

Once you have equipped yourself with some of the key concepts from Chapter Two, the account of personal identities from Chapter Three, the pitfalls of nonfeminist moral theories you encountered in Chapter Four, and the gender-sensitive theories of Chapter Five, you are ready to start doing the close-up work of feminist ethics. Accordingly, Chapter Six offers a close-up of feminist bioethics, Chapter Seven provides a feminist ethical analysis of violence, and Chapter Eight furnishes a close-up of ethical issues arising from the globalized economy, as well as a discussion of cross-cultural ethical judgments.

For Further Reading

Baier, Annette. 1994. *Moral Prejudices: Essays on Ethics.* Cambridge, MA: Harvard University Press.

Beauvoir, Simone de. 1949 [1974]. *The Second Sex.* Trans. and ed. H. M. Parshley. New York: Modern Library.

Hanisch, Carol. 1970. "The Personal Is Political." In *Notes from the Second Year*. New York: Radical Feminism.

Hoagland, Sarah Lucia. 1988. *Lesbian Ethics: Toward New Value.* Palo Alto, CA: Institute of Lesbian Studies.

hooks, bell. 1984. *Feminist Theory from Margin to Center.* Boston: South End Press.

Jaggar, Alison. 1991. "Feminist Ethics: Projects, Problems, Prospects." In *Feminist Ethics,* ed. Claudia Card. Lawrence: University Press of Kansas.

MacKinnon, Catharine A. 1987. *Feminism Unmodified.* Cambridge, MA: Harvard University Press.

Plumwood, Val. 2002. *Environmental Culture: The Ecological Crisis of Reason.* London: Routledge.

Walker, Margaret Urban. 2001. "Seeing Power in Morality: A Proposal for Feminist Naturalism in Ethics." In *Feminists Doing*

Ethics, ed. Peggy DesAutels and Joanne Waugh. Lanham, MD: Rowman & Littlefield.

———. 2003. *Moral Contexts.* Lanham, MD: Rowman & Littlefield.

Wittig, Monique. 1981. "One Is Not Born a Woman." *Feminist Issues* 1, no. 2.

Young, Iris Marion. 1990. *Justice and the Politics of Difference.* Princeton, NJ: Princeton University Press.

CHAPTER

2

Discrimination and Oppression

On 19 June 2001 a class-action sex-discrimination lawsuit was filed in federal court in San Francisco against Wal-Mart Stores, Inc., the largest retailer in the world. The suit alleged that even though three-fourths of the hourly sales employees at Wal-Mart were women, two-thirds of the supervisory and managerial positions were occupied by men, as were nine out of ten of the top store-manager positions. Only one of Wal-Mart's top twenty officers was a woman. Moreover, women working for Wal-Mart were paid an average of 35 cents less an hour than men for entry-level jobs, and because they were promoted much more slowly than men, the wage gap increased over time. By 2001, for example, women who were hired in 1996 were averaging $1.16 less per hour than men who were hired in the same year. The first promotion for men occurred, on average, 2.86 years after the initial hiring, whereas for women it happened after 4.38 years, despite the fact that women's performance ratings for hourly jobs were higher than men's and their turnover rates were lower. Women were denied the training they needed to advance further, and they were almost never told of opportunities for promotion.

A similar class-action lawsuit was brought against Morgan Stanley Dean Witter & Co. on 10 September 2001. The Wall Street brokerage firm was accused of engaging in a pattern of discrimination that prevented most women from advancing to the positions and salaries achieved by men, even when the men were less productive. Among other things, the suit alleged, the men who worked at Morgan Stanley routinely made trips to strip clubs where business was discussed and they brokered deals at golf outings from which women were excluded.

The problem isn't limited to a few bad apples. The General Accounting Office compiled data from the 2000 Current Population Survey regarding the ten sorts of jobs that employ most of the women in the United States, and found that full-time women in management positions earned considerably less than their male counterparts in both 1995 and 2000. The data also revealed that in seven of the ten kinds of jobs examined, the gap in pay actually widened over those years. For example, in 1995 full-time woman managers in the field of communications earned 86 cents for every dollar earned by managers who were men. Five years later, these women earned 73 cents on the dollar.

According to the AFL-CIO's figures for 2004, for every dollar now earned by the average man, the average woman earns 80 cents. If that disparity remains constant, a woman who is 25 years old in 2005 will lose about $455,000 to unequal pay during her working life. Moreover, because women are paid less than men, they have less money to save for their futures and they will earn smaller pensions. Half of all women with income from a pension in 2002 received less than $5,600 per year, compared with $10,340 per year for men. These figures are even worse for women of color: African American women earn only 70 cents and Latinas 59 cents for every dollar that men in general earn.

2.1. Gender Neutrality

One commonsense solution to the problem of gender discrimination is to simply stop discriminating and treat everybody the same. Although, as we saw in Chapter One, the appeal to equality is not without its problems, the ideal of gender neutrality was widespread among feminists in the 1960s and 70s, and it was the moving force behind the efforts, in the 1970s, to ratify the Equal Rights Amendment to the U.S. Constitution. If the amendment had passed (ratification fell short by three states), it would have been unconstitutional for Congress or the state legislatures to use gender as a basis for denying people their rights under the law.

Gender neutrality has been conceived of in two ways: androgyny or assimilation. *Androgyny* has its roots in the Greek words for "man" and "woman," and on this conception, gender neutrality amounts to treating people as if they were neither men nor women, but something in between. The thought is that men and women are the same in more ways than they're different, or at least they could be under the right circumstances, so corporations, judges, legislators, and other policy makers should ignore the physical differences and concentrate on the mental and moral similarities between men and women.

Assimilation, on the other hand, is based on the idea that women really are just like men, or could be if given half a chance. On this conception, gender neutrality dictates that corporations, judges, and lawmakers should treat women in the same way as they already treat men, holding them to the same standards but then also granting them the same privileges. The advantage of assimilation is that it doesn't require radically restructuring society. Existing policies for things like hiring and promotion can be left in place, on the understanding that from now on, women will get the same consideration as men.

However, there are two major drawbacks to gender-neutral policies. One is that they don't respect the relevant ways in which women are *physically* different from men—they just ignore them. There's something slightly ludicrous, for example, about the gender-neutral city ordinance, passed in Texas in the 1970s, that prohibited all firefighters, whether men or women, from breast-feeding their babies between calls. Equally peculiar was the minimum height requirement for airline pilots, which was based on the gender-neutral concern that the pilot needed to be able to reach the control panel, but which failed to recognize that women, who are on average shorter than men, would be able to use the controls if the cockpit were redesigned. At about the same time as these regulations went into effect, advocates of gender neutrality argued that it would be unfair for corporate benefits packages to include maternity leave policies, because they can't be applied "equally" to men.

The second problem with gender neutrality is that it doesn't respect the relevant ways in which women are *socially* different from men: It denies that women lag behind men in the race for the goods that society has to offer. Because gender systematically favors men and disadvantages women, men by and large keep winning that race, while a few women prevail despite carrying a handicap. All that gender-neutral policies do is stop employers from setting extra trip-wires for women or weighting them down further so that they can't run as fast. This helps keep the gap between men and women from widening, but it doesn't narrow it at all. So men go on winning. Built in to gender neutrality is the presumption that the systemwide bias in favor of men has already been eliminated, but in the light of current lawsuits, the reports from the General Accounting Office and the AFL-CIO, and plenty of other evidence, that's just wishful thinking.

2.2. Androcentrism

Another way to put this second criticism of gender-neutral policies is to say that they don't take *androcentrism* into account. Androcentrism is the (usually unstated) view that man is the point of reference for what is normal for human beings. The word, which literally means "men at the center," gives us a different spatial metaphor from the one of a race with the men out front and the women behind. Here the metaphor is that of a circle, with the men in the middle and the women around the circumference. You can think of the circle as the category "human being," where those who stand squarely in the middle are the most fully representative or paradigmatic things of that kind, while the outliers are—well, outliers.

According to androcentrism, the difference from men that pushes women to the margins calls for an explanation, whereas nothing has to be explained about men because they're just normal human beings. Often, the explanation presents women not only as different from men, but as *defective* men. Aristotle, for example, explained that woman is a "mutilated male." The Victorian anthropologist James Allan explained that she is an "undeveloped man." And because regarding man's body as the normal human body tends to produce a view of woman that exaggerates her biological differences from man, it shouldn't surprise us that the nineteenth-century German physician Rudolph Virchow explained woman as "a pair of ovaries with a human being attached, whereas man is a human being furnished with a pair of testicles."

Androcentrism accounts for the lingering use of masculine terminology to stand for generic persons: "The voter exercises his Constitutional rights," "All men are created equal." Androcentrism also accounts for the fact that the supposedly gender-neutral strategy of assimilation requires women to measure up to the male norm rather than requiring men to measure up to women.

Many categories exhibit androcentrism's center-and-margins feature, but they don't all devalue the members of the category that occupy the margin, the way androcentrism does. Think of the category "bird," for instance. If you were asked to draw a picture of a bird you'd probably produce a sketch of something that looks like a robin or a sparrow, but I'll bet you anything that you wouldn't draw a flamingo. That's because robins and sparrows are paradigmatic birds, while flamingoes are outliers. The fact that they're outliers, though, doesn't mean that flamingoes are mutilated robins, or a pair of long legs with a robin attached. The trouble with the category "human being" isn't that it has paradigmatic types and outlier types. It's that gender has infected the category to make it androcentric. As androcentrism sees it, women, not being men, must have something wrong with them. And that being the case, why in the world would Wal-Mart or Morgan Stanley want to promote them?

In the twentieth century, androcentrism was particularly apparent in medical research: Many clinical studies were conducted on male subjects only, on the assumption that men are fully representative human beings. My personal favorite is a pilot study to determine the impact of obesity on breast and ovarian cancer, conducted at Rockefeller University in 1989 *on men alone*. That study raised man-centered medicine to new heights, but it was hardly the only one. Women were typically excluded from experiments to test the safety and efficacy of new drugs, on the grounds that if the women were pregnant the drug could put their fetuses at risk, and anyway, women's hormonal cycles might complicate the picture. But if the drug is tested only on men, how do you know it works the same way in women? And if women's hormonal cycles do in fact complicate the picture, wouldn't you want to know what those complications are? Actually, men have hormonal cycles too, though those have never been characterized as a complication. And that makes the point about androcentrism rather nicely: Men's bodies are the normal ones. It's *women's* bodies that are complicated. And if women are defective men, that complication isn't worth studying.

Racism and discrimination against gays and lesbians employ the same sort of logic: The white race and heterosexuality are the norm for human beings, so anything other than the norm must be defective—not just statistically but *morally* abnormal. Efforts to draw attention away from the group that dominates the center (or, to use yet another spatial metaphor, to dismantle the hierarchy that puts the dominant group on top) will appear, from the perspective of those at the center, as a hostile threat to the group—a threat to "the Southern way of life" or to "the family as we know it." This reaction keeps the focus on the dominant group so that it, rather than the plight of the subgroup, remains the center of attention.

This kind of thinking also operates in global contexts, where it is called *ethnocentrism* (which is like androcentrism applied to cultures). For example, the philosopher Uma Narayan argues in *Dislocated Cultures* (1997, 136–42) that in the global North, people often treat Southern countries as mirrors of the North, seeing India, Africa, South America, and so on essentially as places where Northern imperialism and colonialism have played themselves out. This, she says, is a strategy that permits Northerners to take an interest in the global South without having to come to know that world on its own terms, because the critical perspective is confined to *Northern* interference, exploitation, images, and the like. The attention is deflected from others to Us: what's important is Us wringing our hands, not what life is like for people in the global South. (This is an instance of Lindemann's ad hoc rule Number 63: The most important question, always, is "What do *you* think about me?")

2.3. Affirmative Action

It seems, then, that because gender-neutral policies ignore the androcentrism that keeps the spotlight on men's bodies, needs, career patterns, concerns, preoccupations, and conquests, they can't get at the underlying causes of gender discrimination in the workplace and elsewhere. As women don't seem to receive the right kind of help from policies that treat everyone the same, the next logical place to look is at policies that treat different groups differently. Affirmative action policies do just that: They single out underrepresented groups for corrective efforts at inclusion. Most of the recent discussion about affirmative action has involved court cases where race was at issue rather than gender, but as race is gendered and gender has racial implications, it's worth looking at the arguments for and against such policies.

In April 2003 the U.S. Supreme Court heard oral arguments in two cases challenging the constitutionality of the University of Michigan's use of affirmative action in its admissions programs. *Grutter v. Bollinger* concerned admissions to the university's Law School, while *Gratz v. Bollinger* dealt with admissions to its undergraduate College of Literature, Science, and the Arts. In both cases, the plaintiffs were white applicants who were turned away even though minority students with lower test scores were admitted. Both sets of plaintiffs argued that the university's race-conscious admissions process unlawfully discriminated against them.

The legal precedent for the Michigan cases is an earlier Supreme Court decision, *Regents of the University of California v. Bakke* (1978). That case involved the admissions program to the University of California Medical School at Davis. Out of an entering class of 100, the medical school set aside 16 spaces for students admitted through a special program for minority applicants. A majority of the Supreme Court (five justices) held that while the University of California's admissions program was unconstitutional because it involved a quota, it was nevertheless lawful to take race into account in the admissions process. Justice Lewis F. Powell, who offered the narrowest ground supporting the use of race in college admissions, wrote the controlling opinion of the Court. He found that the educational benefits of *diversity* were a compelling governmental interest justifying the use of race as a "plus factor" in admissions, adding that race can be considered as one of many factors that may influence admissions decisions when the university is trying to achieve overall diversity.

Before *Grutter v. Bollinger* reached the Supreme Court, it was heard by the Sixth Circuit Court of Appeals. That court, guided by the *Bakke* decision, duly ruled that diversity is a compelling interest and that the Law School's admissions policy is narrowly tailored to serve that interest. The court found that the Law School's pursuit of a "critical mass" of students from underrepresented groups provides a class with meaningful numbers of minority students so as "to ensure that all students—majority and minority alike—will be able to enjoy the educational benefits of a diverse student body." It added that the Law School had ample reason to decide that some consideration of race is necessary to achieve its goal of a diverse student body. In June 2003 the Supreme Court agreed. In *Gratz v. Bollinger,* the Supreme Court decided that undergraduate racial criteria weren't as narrowly tailored as the Law School's, so it struck them down.

The diversity argument for affirmative action certainly seems to address the problem of androcentrism, since members of a dominant group who regularly interact with members of minority groups are likely to learn that the world doesn't revolve around them. Unfortunately, this is another one of those areas where appearances can be deceiving. If you look carefully at who has to do what for this learning to take place, you'll notice that despite the Sixth Circuit's talk of "majority and minority alike," the majority and minority play very different roles here. Minorities already know a lot about majority culture—they have to, if they're going to survive in it. By contrast, an important way in which majorities are privileged is that they don't have to know anything about minority cultures. So, while diversity on college campuses has something to offer the majority, minority students are far less likely to benefit from it. In fact, minority students are expected to *supply* the benefit, by explaining to students in the majority what minority life is like. Minority students will, in effect, be treated as a kind of curriculum enrichment program whose purpose is to educate the members of the majority. But do we really want to say that the primary reason for having minority students on campus is so that they can do unpaid teaching? If what justifies their presence on campus is that they will provide this service, should they be turned away if they don't deliver? And why is it *their* job to help majority students overcome their racism or sexism? The diversity argument looks as if it benefits everybody, but it actually stays focused on the dominant group: the gaps in the dominant group's education, what the dominant group needs, how the dominant group can be helped, why this would be good for the dominant group. There's more than a whiff of ethnocentrism to the Sixth Circuit's rationale for diversity among the student body.

This criticism is not meant to imply that diversity is a bad idea or that members of minority groups don't also benefit from making connections and forming friendships with members of the socially dominant group. Policies that include minorities are better than those that don't, provided that the inclusion doesn't come with a certificate of second-class citizenship. And the argument for diversity may have the best chance, politically, of gaining widespread acceptance for affirmative action programs. What the criticism highlights, however, is that there are unsavory assumptions built in to the diversity argument that aren't easily detected. It also highlights how hard it is to tear one's eyes away from the center, even with the best of intentions.

A more frequently voiced criticism of affirmative action programs is that they hurt minorities by making it look as if they can't succeed without help. "Actually," the office workers mutter to themselves, "she only got that promotion because she's a woman." Or, said of a black woman entering a prestigious law firm, "Well, *that* was an affirmative action hire." In a racist and sexist society, many people assume that anyone from the (defective) margins who moves closer to the (privileged) middle of her culture is still defective and therefore not really entitled to the money, prestige, or other good things that those in the middle enjoy. She is still overly emotional, or bitchy, or too sexually attractive to do the job as well as a man can. And if she's black, Latina, disabled, or lesbian, she's also ____________ (fill in your favorite stereotype). There is a stigma attached to affirmative action. It's perceived as a handout for people who aren't good enough to make it on their own.

2.4. The Dilemma of Difference

So now we have a problem. It seems that when we treat all people the same, we don't address the patterns of discrimination that accompany group differences. And when we treat people differently, we reinforce those selfsame patterns of discrimination. The feminist legal scholar Martha Minow dubs this problem "the dilemma of difference," and she poses it in the form of two questions: "When does treating people differently emphasize their differences and stigmatize or hinder them on that basis? And when does treating people the same become insensitive to their difference and likely to stigmatize or hinder them on that basis?" (Minow 1990, 20). The dilemma is a classic double bind: The stigma of being different can be perpetuated both by ignoring difference and by focusing on it. And if Minow is right about this, it's a dim outlook for those women at Wal-Mart.

Catharine A. MacKinnon argues that you'll never get rid of the stigma if you stay focused on difference, because accepting a person or group as different actually *hides* the fact that any discrimination is going on. That, she says, is what happened in *Plessy v. Ferguson* (1896), where the Supreme Court ruled that racially segregated railroad cars were lawful under the "separate but equal" doctrine. "If you see Black people as different," she points out, "there is no harm to segregation; it is merely a recognition of that difference" (MacKinnon 1987, 178). The fact that black people are *disadvantaged* when they are segregated—when, for example, black children have to attend substandard schools—won't be visible as harm, because the schools won't be seen as substandard. They'll just be seen as different. In the same way, if the gap in earnings between men and women is just perceived as one of the differences between them, the fact that poverty makes a real and disproportionate impact on women's lives won't be registered as a harm.

To stop gender discrimination in the workplace (or anywhere else, for that matter), you first have to notice, rather than cover up, the fact that women aren't just being treated differently. As MacKinnon puts it, if gender is just a matter of difference, then nothing is wrong. But if gender is a matter of a *power* relation that systematically subordinates women to men, then "the issue is not the gender difference but the difference gender makes" (MacKinnon 1987, 176). The difference that gender makes, of course, is that it creates an unjust hierarchy, and while you can talk about the difference between the top and the bottom of the hierarchy, what distinguishes the top from the bottom isn't "difference"—it's power.

And that's precisely what the "diversity" rationale for affirmative action misses. The Sixth Circuit arguably did just what the *Plessy* court did, in that it focused on difference while ignoring the systematic subordination of black people to white. It didn't acknowledge that the two groups are caught up in a power system that puts white people on top and black people on the bottom, where they don't have equal access to the opportunities, benefits, and privileges that white people enjoy. When the courts stay focused on diversity, they do nothing to remedy the harm and injustice done to the group on the bottom. What they ignore, in short, is the fact of oppression.

2.5. Oppression

The feminist philosopher Marilyn Frye (1983) defines the oppression of women as a network of "forces and barriers that expose one to penalty, loss or contempt whether one works outside the home or not, is on welfare or not, bears children or not, raises children or not, marries or not, stays married or not, is heterosexual, lesbian, both or neither" (3). The experience of oppression, she says, is that of confinement by obstacles that aren't accidental or occasional or avoidable, but are "systematically related to each other in such a way as to catch one between and among them and restrict or penalize motion in any direction" (4). Her well-known image of oppression is that of a birdcage. If you look carefully at just one wire of the cage (for example, not being told about opportunities for promotion), you won't be able to see why the bird couldn't just fly around the wire any time it wanted to go somewhere. And if, on the following days, you look just as carefully at each of the other wires, you'll still be baffled by the bird's inability to move. It's only if you step back and notice how each wire is connected to the other wires, all of which work together to form a cage, that you see—instantly—why the bird doesn't go anywhere.

Oppression is a system of institutional forces and processes that keep the members of some social groups from full participation in their society. It prevents group members from learning or using valuable skills. It hampers their access to jobs, housing, and the other material goods the society has to offer. It withholds from them the authority to speak knowledgeably about their feelings or points of view. It denies that their experience is real, which produces what the African American scholar and activist W. E. B. Du Bois called "double consciousness"—the sense of always looking at yourself through the eyes of others, but refusing to accept the stereotyped, devalued, and stigmatized view of yourself that they see.

The Five Faces of Oppression

Iris Marion Young, noting that oppressed groups are oppressed in different ways, suggests that oppression names a family of concepts and conditions, not all of which will necessarily play the same sort of role in every case. She divides these concepts and conditions into five "faces," or manifestations, of oppression: exploitation, marginalization, powerlessness, cultural imperialism, and violence.

Exploitation. Following Karl Marx's lead, Young (1990) understands exploitation as "a steady process of the transfer of the results of the labor of one social group to benefit another" (49). Unlike Marx, though, Young thinks that exploitation involves more than an unjust distribution of goods and services—it also involves an unjust social structure, which dictates how the products of some people's work are to be taken over by other people. Young argues that while women are exploited in the Marxist sense to the degree that they work for wages, they're also exploited by corporate and domestic institutions which, while failing to acknowledge or even to notice it, require women "to benefit men by releasing them for more important and creative work, enhancing their status or the environment around them, or providing them with sexual or emotional service" (51). Similarly, African Americans as a group are exploited because the labor market tends to reserve unionized, well-paying, interesting jobs for whites, on the assumption that African Americans and members of other nonwhite racial groups ought to be the servants or assistants of the people who enjoy race privilege. Social *processes* unfairly transfer the products of one group's labor to another, and social *institutions* allow the few to acquire wealth while preventing the many from doing so. Exploitation causes groups of people to be identified primarily as resources for other people, requiring them to serve these others' interests.

Marginalization. This face of oppression refers to the exclusion of particular social groups from useful participation in social life. The marginalized are the groups of people the system of labor can't or won't use. "In the United States," Young (1990) writes, "a shamefully large proportion of the population is marginal: old people, and increasingly people who are not very old but get laid off from their jobs and cannot find new work; young people, especially Black or Latino, who cannot find first or second jobs; many single mothers and their children; other people involuntarily unemployed; many mentally and physically disabled people; American Indians, especially those on reservations" (53). Because groups like these are considered useless, they either can't find work or don't get paid for the work they do, and as a result they suffer from poverty. Some even face extinction. Marginalization causes groups of people to be identified primarily as unwanted or undesirable, depriving them of an important source of hope.

Powerlessness. Just as the class division between capitalist and worker displays the face of exploitation, so, according to Young, the class division between professional and nonprofessional reveals the face of powerlessness. Where professionals receive the university education that allows them to advance in a career and to achieve increasingly higher levels of social recognition, nonprofessionals have to work in jobs that tend to go nowhere in particular and lack status. Where professionals often set their own hours and decide for themselves what task to do next, nonprofessionals have to answer to professionals and are continually supervised by them. And because professionals and nonprofessionals tend to live in different neighborhoods, have different tastes, and have different amounts of disposable income, the privileges of the professional extend beyond the workplace to nearly all aspects of social life.

Young calls the professional's way of life "respectability." As a rule, professionals expect and receive more respect than nonprofessionals get. Professionals, for example, don't have to pass drug tests as a condition of employment. Professionals don't see police cars cruising by their houses several times a night. Professionals don't punch time clocks. Professionals don't wear uniforms with the company logo on them. Because professionalism commands respect, "nonprofessionals seeking a loan or a job, or to buy a house or a car, will often try to look 'professional' and 'respectable' in those settings" (Young 1990, 58). Powerlessness causes groups of people to be identified primarily as disreputable and untrustworthy, requiring them to be supervised by others.

Cultural Imperialism. While exploitation, marginalization, and powerlessness are largely a matter of concrete power relations stemming from the economic arrangements that determine who gets to work, what kind of work they get to do, and who is supposed to work for whom, cultural imperialism refers to the power relation that obtains when a dominant group's way of life becomes the standard against which other groups' ways of doing things are judged. "Cultural imperialism involves the universalization of a dominant group's experience and culture, and its establishment as the norm" (Young 1990, 59). Sound familiar? It should. Cultural imperialism is Young's term for what I earlier called ethnocentrism, and it works the same way androcentrism does: The dominant group takes its own experiences, achievements, and values to be representative of human nature per se. Using its own standards to judge other groups—standards to which those others don't conform—the dominant group regretfully or triumphantly or unthinkingly concludes that the other groups can't quite make the grade. Cultural imperialism causes groups of people to be identified primarily as defective human beings, depriving them of social standing and self-respect.

Violence. Members of many groups live in fear of attacks that are motivated by nothing but the dominant group's desire to humiliate, hurt, or destroy them. Young includes the less severe practices of harassment, intimidation, and ridicule in this category as well, when their sole purpose is to degrade people belonging to social groups that don't fit the dominant norms. Violence of this kind is systemic, because it's directed at people simply because they are members of a despised group. It's social, because people often band together to do it (in gang rape, for example) and because there are rules about when the target of the violence has asked for it (he got uppity, she was in the wrong neighborhood). And although there's a limit beyond which this kind of violence isn't tolerated, up to that limit it *is* tolerated. People know it will happen again, frequently, and so they become used to it. Its perpetrators often receive light punishment or none at all, particularly if they are in positions of authority. Violence causes groups of people to be identified primarily as objects of sport or hatred, requiring them to take responsibility for their own safety.

The Four Forces of Oppression

Where Frye offers the image of a birdcage and Young speaks of five "faces," I see oppression in terms of the crosscurrents and undertows that circulate through society, pushing the members of social groups this way and that with respect to the dominant group. I've identified four such forces, some or all of which might be present in any given form of oppression, though you could perhaps think of other forces to add to this list (Nelson 2001, 112–17).

The first force is *pressive:* The group is pressed into serving members of the dominant group. Consider, for example, a patriarchal marriage in a society that doesn't permit women to own property and also forbids divorce. Pressive forces compel the wife to serve her husband, and they also establish norms for how she is supposed to do it. She must meet his sexual needs, care for his children, keep his house clean, defer to him, enter into no relationships with other men, and so on. The penalty for failure to comply with these norms can be quite severe. She might be raped by her husband if she's not willing to have sex, have her children taken away by the state or other family members if she doesn't provide all their care, be beaten if she doesn't defer to her husband, be stoned for adultery if she takes a lover. If she refuses the relationship by running away, she'll become a social outcast and, having no money of her own, add starvation to her other miseries. If, on the other hand, she is a compliant wife, then although her husband might still harm her, she has a reason to trust that he won't—particularly if they both believe that his authority over her is morally justified. And just as she trusts that her husband won't harm her if she lives up to the norms, so too he trusts her—he entrusts himself, his house, and his children into her care. When such trust is absent, this particular power arrangement can't hold.

The second force is *expulsive:* The group is driven out of the larger society. The example that first comes to mind is Nazi Germany, where the aim was to expel Jews, Gypsies, Jehovah's Witnesses, gays and lesbians, disabled people, Communists, and other folk not fit to live in the Third Reich. Expulsive forces don't set up a relationship the way that pressive forces do. Where the object is genocide, no relationship is desired or allowed. Instead, the dominant group refuses to tolerate the presence of the other group in the larger society and is interested in neither the group members' own view of the matter nor in any sort of mutual accommodation.

The third force is *dismissive:* The group is tolerated on the fringes of the larger society, where it can remain as long as its members don't lay claim to the goods and opportunities that are enjoyed by those in the dominant group. So, for example, ageism pushes the elderly out on the margins of social life but doesn't, for the most part, insist on killing them. Native Americans are pushed onto reservations; the homeless are pushed to live under bridges; gays are pushed into their closets without actually being expelled outright. The point of abusive power arrangements fueled by dismissive forces is that the dominant group should have as little to do with the other group as possible. The dominant group doesn't want the other group to serve its members; it wants the other group to stay out of its way. And so it polices the group to make sure that it remains marginalized. Because dismissive forces keep the group at arm's length, the degree of trust required to sustain the power relation is minimal.

The fourth is *preservative:* The dominant group considers this group abnormal, which keeps its sense of what is normal in place. In social arrangements that enforce a strict system of gender, for example, women are expected to desire men and men to desire women; heterosexual desire is a part of what it means to be a woman or a man in these arrangements. The preservative forces that flow through the gender system police desire. Unlike pressive forces, preservative forces don't require a group to perform services for heterosexuals—they insist that all people *be* heterosexual. If some men and women refuse, the preservative forces push them into the role of Other, stigmatizing them so that they pose less of a threat to the gender system. The preservative forces ensure not only that gender continues to be the identification with one sex, but also that it continues to require that sexual desire is directed toward the other sex. Gays, lesbians, and bisexuals thus become the "not-us" that allows "us" to keep on defining itself in heterosexual terms.

2.6. Back to Gender Discrimination

Oppression, then, can be described in terms of its power to immobilize, its five faces or manifestations, or the forces by which it operates. And as my criticisms of the diversity argument and of gender-neutral strategies suggest, it's oppression, not discrimination, that is at the root of the trouble at Morgan Stanley and Wal-Mart. Discriminatory policies can cause or perpetuate oppression, but what makes those policies wrong is that they are oppressive, not that they discriminate.

Equivocation between two senses of 'discrimination' has caused a lot of confusion, so it's important for us to be as clear about them as possible. Here's a form of discrimination: inviting only your friends to your party. Here's another: U.S. citizenship. Used this way, discrimination means consciously preferring some people rather than others on the basis of their group membership—something that isn't in itself immoral. But when people talk about 'gender discrimination,' they're using the term in a very different sense. This kind of discrimination is *unfair,* because it consists of the biases and prejudices that disadvantage women and privilege men.

When a group of city officials and businessmen exclude women from their monthly lunch meetings, their discriminating against women is wrong because it reinforces networks of privilege and opportunities that already exist for men and that harm women. On the other hand, when a group of professional women exclude men from gatherings designed to counteract the sense of isolation and strain the women experience as unwelcome minorities in their fields, their discrimination against men is not wrong, because it serves the purpose of *undermining* the oppression of their group. As Young (1990) puts it, "If discrimination serves the purpose of undermining the oppression of a group, it may be not only permitted, but morally required" (197).

Whether discrimination is wrong depends entirely on the reason for doing it. That being the case, it's no real criticism of affirmative action to complain that it's "reverse discrimination." What would be a problem is if an affirmative action policy produced reverse racism or sexism. To do that, though, the policy would have to turn the current patterns of oppression upside down: Women would consistently outearn men; African American skin color, hair, and facial features would be thought of as normal; you'd naturally assume an administrative assistant was a man. Honk if you think that's going to happen anytime soon.

Feminist ethics offers different ways of understanding and responding to the damage done by hiring and promotion patterns that are biased against women. One such response is to implement affirmative action policies, not on the grounds that they promote diversity, but because they intervene in the process of oppression. When companies and other institutions use these policies, they're announcing their acceptance of women in positions other than at the cash register or the copy machine. They're helping themselves to the advantage of having women participate in decision-making bodies, where their experiences and concerns, being rather different from those of most men, can provide important perspectives that were previously not available. And most important of all, they're countering the institutional prejudices that keep women from exercising their full potential.

In this chapter we have examined some of the tools that are found in the feminist ethicist's toolkit: the concepts of gender neutrality, androcentrism and its cousin ethnocentrism, difference, and oppression. In the next chapter we'll look at how gender interacts with other power systems to shape people's personal identities. Because our identities set up socially normative expectations for how we are supposed to behave and how other sorts of people may treat us, it's important for feminist ethicists to understand the role that gender plays in our own and others' sense of who we are.

For Further Reading

Frye, Marilyn. 1983. *The Politics of Reality: Essays in Feminist Theory.* Freedom, CA: Crossing Press.

Lindemann, Hilde. See Nelson, Hilde Lindemann.

MacKinnon, Catharine A. 1987. *Feminism Unmodified.* Cambridge, MA: Harvard University Press.

Minow, Martha. 1990. *Making All the Difference: Inclusion, Exclusion, and American Law.* Ithaca, NY: Cornell University Press.

Narayan, Uma. 1997. *Dislocating Cultures: Identities, Traditions, and Third World Feminism.* New York: Routledge.

Nelson, Hilde Lindemann. 2001. *Damaged Identities, Narrative Repair.* Ithaca, NY: Cornell University Press.

Young, Iris Marion. 1990. *Justice and the Politics of Difference.* Princeton, NJ: Princeton University Press.

CHAPTER
3

The Importance of Who We Are

You meet your friends at the local watering hole and order a beer, and the waiter cards you. You're about to go through the security check at the airport, and the agent asks you for a photo ID. You're driving down the expressway, you get pulled over for speeding, and the state trooper demands to see your driver's license. In all these instances you are, in effect, being asked a question about your identity—one that the philosopher Marya Schechtman has dubbed the "reidentification question." This is a question about whether you, at this particular point in time, are the *same as* the person who was born long enough ago to drink legally, or was issued the plane ticket, or passed the driving test.

Nonfeminist philosophers who think about identity have spent a lot of time and energy on the reidentification question, developing and defending various criteria for determining when—or whether—a person at one point in time is the same as the person at an earlier or later point in time. And it's an interesting question. It's useful, for example, to know whether the man now standing before the judge is the same person as the one who committed the burglary last week, or whether the youth now claiming to be the long-lost Prince of Ruritania is the same person as the baby who was kidnapped from his cradle years ago by the king's enemies. It's also fun to play with the various science-fiction versions of the question that philosophers have dreamed up. For instance, if my brain were transplanted into somebody else's body, and my body received somebody else's brain, would either of the two resulting people still be me?

Feminist ethicists have also been greatly concerned with questions of personal identity, but they are less interested in the reidentification question than in what Schechtman calls the "characterization question." This is a question, not about whether a person at one point in time is identical with some person at another point in time, but about *who* a person is. It's the question about how a person thinks, feels, and acts, what matters to her, how she sees herself, and how others act toward her. It's the "Who am I?" that might be asked by a victim of amnesia or by someone in the throes of an identity crisis.

Why are feminist ethicists so interested in issues of personal identity? Let's divide this question into two parts. First, we can ask what's so important from a *feminist* point of view about who someone is (this part of the question will take a little explanation). Second, we can ask why personal identities are important for feminist *ethics*.

From a feminist perspective, an obvious reason for the focus on personal identities in the sense of the characterization question is that feminism is about gender and gender is an important component of people's identities. So feminists have to pay attention, at the very least, to whether a person is a man or a woman or in between. But they can't stop there. In fact, when they have restricted themselves to considerations of gender alone, abstracting it from the other particulars that contribute to our identities, they have generally gotten themselves into trouble. As the philosopher Elizabeth V. Spelman (1988) puts it, "The attempt to isolate gender from other elements of human identity such as race and class . . . has been instrumental in the preservation of white middle-class privilege in feminist theory" (16).

Here's an example of the kind of thing she means. In the early 1960s, Betty Friedan (1963) wrote a book about "the problem that has no name," which "lay buried, unspoken, for many years in the minds of American women" (15). The problem, which she dubbed "the feminine mystique," was that women were made seriously unhappy by their unfulfilling, stay-at-home lives as suburban housewives and mothers. The solution, Friedan declared, was to "hire a cleaning woman," get out of the house, and take a paid job. In its day, *The Feminine Mystique* was both controversial and influential, and it has earned a prominent place in the annals of American feminism. But it also does a great job of reproducing white, middle-class privilege.

Think for a moment about the "American woman" as Friedan envisions her. First of all, she's a wife, and since she doesn't have to work outside the home, her husband presumably earns enough money to support her. She lives in the suburbs, not in an inner-city apartment. The job she expects to get isn't likely to be a factory job or service work, since it promises to fulfill her. And her home is a trap that makes her restless, not a place where she can recover from and resist the brutal social forces of the larger society. She is not poor. She is not uneducated. She is most certainly not, herself, a cleaning woman. She is not an African American woman, not a Latina, not a lesbian.

Sounds pretty white, married, and middle-class, doesn't she? And that would be fine if Friedan had intentionally restricted her focus to discontented white, middle-class housewives. But she didn't. She was speaking about American women in the abstract, as if gender could be separated from race, class, ethnic heritage, and the other elements that make up a person's identity. As there *are* no American women in the abstract, however, Friedan ended up filling in those other elements by writing as if all women—all the ones who counted, anyway—were discontented white, middle-class housewives. There's an analogy here to androcentrism. Just as gender sets men up as the norm for human beings, so other power arrangements set up their favored groups as the norm. Like androcentrism, the assumption that the concerns of white, middle-class women are somehow more real than anyone else's tends to make other groups of women invisible. If you think 'women' should work outside the home, you aren't paying attention to the many women who are already working outside the home because they have no choice.

That's what Spelman calls "privilege." Privilege means not having to notice or think about people who aren't like you. It means that your kind of person counts, but other kinds don't count. Often, privilege is taken for granted rather than malicious: We needn't suppose that Friedan was deliberately trying to insult the women who clean other people's houses by implying that they themselves weren't women. But we can fault her for focusing so hard on 'femininity' that she forgot about the other components of people's identities. As a result, those components crept in the back door while she wasn't looking.

Since Friedan's time, white, heterosexual, middle-class feminists have tried hard not to make that mistake. They have learned, as Spelman (1988) puts it, that "the more universal the claim one might hope to make about women—'women have been put on a pedestal' or 'women have been treated like slaves'—the more likely it is to be false. If we think of women who were part of slave populations, their problem surely was not that they were put on a pedestal; and it would be very odd to say that they were 'treated like slaves' if they *were* slaves" (8). The feminists who didn't already know it have learned that they can't lump all women together as if there were no differences among them. They have learned, in short, that they have to pay attention to the variety of social group identities from which our personal identities draw many of their features.

Personal identities in the sense of the characterization question are important to *ethics* because they set up certain expectations: They convey understandings of what those who bear them are expected to do. If an answer to "Who are you?" is "a hermit," I expect you to leave me alone; if the answer is "a used-car salesman," I don't. Moreover, identities also convey a sense of how those who bear them may expect to be treated. If you're my three-year-old son, I can remind you to use the toilet, but if you're my boss, I'd better not. Personal identities make intelligible to us, then, not only how various groups of people are supposed to act, but also how well or badly other groups may treat them. I'll have a great deal more to say about the ethical implications of this later in the chapter, but first it might be just as well if I explained in greater detail what feminist ethicists mean by a personal identity.

3.1. What Is a Personal Identity?

As the feminist philosopher Cheshire Calhoun points out, the term *identity* is ambiguous. She identifies three things it could mean (Calhoun 2000, 19). First, it can refer to the social category that people occupy (or that other people think they occupy), such as lesbian, student, or Presbyterian. Second, it can refer to "the subjective experience of living with a particular identity and to the subjective meaning that that identity has for oneself"—for example, what it means to you to live as a black man and how you interpret what being black does and doesn't involve. Third, it can mean a culturally authorized understanding of social difference, such as the difference between management and labor or between boy and girl. My own view is that 'identity' means all these things at once. Your identity is a complicated interplay of how you see yourself and how others see you, and both senses of who you are take some of their shape from culturally authorized, shared understandings of what sorts of lives there are and who may (or must) live them.

As a provisional definition, this already hints at one of the features of personal identities on which many feminists agree: Identities are *social constructions.* They are *multiple:* People have more than one at a time. They are *relational*—that is, they are always connected to other identities within a social web. They are *often unchosen.* And to this list I would add: They are *narratively constituted.* Let's consider each of these features in turn.

Identities Are Social Constructions

To call something a social construction is to say that it's a social fact rather than a natural fact. A social construction is a human achievement, but it takes more than one human being to bring it into existence—it takes a whole society. In Chapter One I argued that gender is a social construction; so is the English language; so is the Internet. Identities are social constructions in that they're created by the concrete practices and institutions of a given way of living—what Ludwig Wittgenstein calls a "form of life." Being a used-car salesman, to advert to an earlier example, is not a possible identity if, in your culture, camels are the only mode of transportation. Likewise, to be a samurai warrior requires a samurai culture—not just a warrior class, but the proper form of aristocracy and all the trappings that support it. As

Calhoun (2000) puts it when writing about gay identities, "By supplying meaningful content to a concept of homosexuality, and a script for enacting a homosexual identity, a culture creates the opportunity for individuals to be homosexual in much the same way that a culture can create the opportunity for individuals to be a peasant or a Democrat" (20).

The form of life not only creates the possibility for *enacting* a given identity—it also, as Calhoun indicates, determines what that identity *means.* It does this by situating the identity within its own broader, socially constructed meaning systems. In the current American form of life the identity of 'mother,' for example, means what it does because of the role within Christianity of the Virgin Mary, the wicked stepmothers of children's nursery tales, the commercial aspects of Mother's Day, the association with God and apple pie, Al Jolson in blackface singing "Mammy," and on and on and on.

Identities Are Multiple

Who we are is never just one thing. We all have a number of ways of describing ourselves, and because we act on the basis of these descriptions, the philosopher Christine Korsgaard (1996) calls them our practical identities: "You are a human being, a woman or a man, an adherent of a certain religion, a member of an ethnic group, a member of a certain profession, someone's lover or friend, and so on. And all of these identities give rise to reasons and obligations" (101).

Much of our lives consists in juggling our different identities: Your professional identity gives you a reason to stay late at the office, but your identity as a marathoner gives you a reason to shut the computer down and go for a run. As a soldier, you obey orders, but as a morally competent adult you don't obey the order to commit a war crime. These are cases where different practical identities conflict temporarily or in a way that can be resolved, but there are also cases where the conflict is permanent. Here I am not thinking of multiple personality disorder or other forms of mental illness but, rather, of identities that aren't compatible because the forms of life that sustain them rule each other out. The philosopher María Lugones talks about these forms of life as different "worlds." One of her own "worlds" is the Latin American culture in which she grew up and in which her relatives still live; another of her "worlds" is her U.S. lesbian community. Her Latin "world" views homosexuality as sinful and wrong, while her lesbian "world" doesn't speak Spanish and can't enter into her Latina heritage. Although her Latina and lesbian identities are incompatible, she affirms them both, shifting from one to the other in a movement she calls "'world'-travelling." Similarly, the lesbian feminist poet Gloria Anzaldúa writes about the "borderlands" inhabited by the people of Mexican origin who live in the southwestern United States. Their Mexican heritage, heavily influenced by Aztec culture and by Roman Catholicism, is already a hybrid identity, but it's overlaid with the culture of their Anglo colonizers. Add the borders between upper and lower class, between white and mixed race, between *machismo* and feminism, between women-oriented women and men-oriented women, and you have the borderlands—a place that's riddled with contradictions.

Identities Are Relational

Part of what it means to say that identities are social constructions is that we always are who we are in relation to other people. As Margaret Urban Walker (1998) puts it, "Our identities, moral and otherwise, are produced by and in histories of specific relationship" (113). Nearly all feminist accounts of personal identity have focused on the way persons are formed in relation to others and sustained in a social context. In Annette Baier's (1985) words, persons are always "second persons"—they are "essentially successors, heirs to other persons who formed and cared for them" (84).

To see what she means, imagine that Rachel, young and poor, surrenders her child at birth to an enormously wealthy couple who live in a mansion on Chicago's Magnificent Mile. Now imagine an alternative story: Rachel keeps the child and rears him in an Orthodox Jewish community in Brownsville, New York. Finally, imagine that Rachel and her child win a trip to Brazil, and when their plane crashes in the Amazon basin, the child survives and is adopted by aboriginal people living in the rain forest much as their ancestors did. Same child, three very different futures. Surely we would want to say that the identity of the man who this child grows up to be is hugely dependent on the identities of the people who formed and cared for him in whichever of the three contexts he was reared. In each of those three different "worlds," Rachel's child would be a different person.

Identities Are Often Unchosen

The philosopher Claudia Card argues that identities aren't always a matter of choice. She has been told, she writes, that her ancestry is Scots, though she doesn't voluntarily identify with that ethnicity. "I love music but have a low tolerance for bagpipes. I like plaids but do not wear skirts, not even kilts. And I seem not to have inherited proverbial Scottish attitudes toward money." Nevertheless, she speculates that her sensibilities, dispositions, attitudes, and values might well be inherited from her Scots ancestors. "If such influences are transmitted through the parenting process, and if they construct me ethnically, my ethnicity may have little to do with my choices or voluntary identifications. Being an ethnic Scot may be part of my moral luck" (Card 1995, 146).

Much of who we are is a matter of luck, as the example of Rachel's child reveals. If you're an American, it's usually not because you chose to be, but because your parents happen to be Americans and you inherited their citizenship. It's a matter of luck whether you are a sister or a brother, and for lots of people, being a parent is a matter of luck too, though they might have chosen the activity that ultimately gave birth to this identity. The color of your skin and what that means, whether you are rich or poor, disabled or able-bodied, Muslim or atheist, intellectually bright or dull-witted—these aspects of your identity are largely matters over which you have little control.

Many identities are not only unchosen but socially forced on us as well. In *Gender Trouble,* the postmodern theorist Judith Butler argues that 'woman' is an identity of that kind—it's a compulsory performance, acted out according to a social script that imposes the identity on bodies that are sexed female. Social pressures "write" the identity on the surface of the body, forcing it into high heels, for example, or causing it to shave its legs and underarms. The same social pressures push the body into the correct positions for walking and sitting like a woman, getting in and out of a car gracefully, throwing a baseball like a girl. (This is an example of Lindemann's ad hoc rule Number 47: When millions of people think women look good in skirts but men look ridiculous, it's not because they took a vote.) 'Woman,' in other words, is an identity that you "do," and you do it so repeatedly that you come to think that your womanliness is inside you instead of molded onto you. You have a fair amount of discretion as to just *how* you end up doing 'woman' (maybe you've pitched a shut-out and never worn heels in your life), but as any teenage girl will tell you, the pressure to perform your gender properly is enormous and unremitting.

Identities Are Narratively Constituted

Some feminist ethicists (including me) have argued that identities consist of a tissue of stories that represent who the person is over time. On this view, your identity isn't you—it's the *depiction* of you that you and other people use to make sense of who you are. And because what needs to be made sense of is your life over time, the depiction can't be thought of as a snapshot that shows who you are only in a given moment. Instead, an identity consists of stories that weave together one moment with the next moment and the moment after that, capturing the ways you change, as well as the ways you stay the same. Many of the stories in the narrative tissue that constitutes your identity are first-person stories, the ones that depict you from your own point of view. But because none of us has total control over who we are or want to be, a number of the stories in that tissue are second- and third-person stories—the ones that other people use to make sense of you.

Identity-constituting stories aren't just *depictive*—they're *selective*. Rather than representing every moment of your life, they cluster around the things about you that matter the most to you, as well as around the things about you that matter the most to other people. These aren't necessarily the same. Your Muslim ancestry, for example, might not matter very much to you at all, especially if, many years before you were born, your family was assimilated into the Christian culture you now live in. But if that culture is the United States, you'll find your ancestry matters a great deal to the security guards at the airport who suspect you of ties to al Qaeda. Because identities are often unchosen, the things about you that other people choose to emphasize might have a far greater impact on your life than your own, first-person stories do.

It's because identity-constituting stories are also *interpretive* that they can serve as a guide to your future as well as making sense of your past. Suppose your father has just had a debilitating heart attack and your mother is struggling to keep the family business going. You know she'd like you to come home and take over the business, but to do that, you'd have to give up your scholarship to a world-class music conservatory and postpone, perhaps for many years, your dream of becoming a professional singer. Walker has argued in *Moral Contexts* (2003, 5–12) that in situations of this kind, where either option is morally permissible, you can engage in "strong moral self-definition." You begin by reviewing your personal history, weighing it in terms of general values ("Do my past actions show that I care about my family?" "When I think of how I've spent my time, can I really say that music is my life?"). Then you either ratify that history and remain on your present course, or repudiate it and set yourself a new course ("I've never appreciated my parents the way I should. I'm not going to keep letting them do all the giving while I do all the taking."). Either way, you create a moral track record that commits you to certain values for the future. The review of your history is a backward-looking story that lets you interpret who you've been. The commitment to a future course of action is a forward-looking story that shows you where you want to go. Using both kinds of stories to make your decision allows certain personal features of your life to matter though they wouldn't necessarily matter for someone else, and in this way you purposefully and deliberately shape your own identity.

Finally, identity-constituting stories are *connective*. They draw connections both within themselves, tying together various actions, events, and personalities into a comprehensible whole, and to other stories. Many of the local, particular stories that contribute to your identity are connected to the widely known, socially shared master narratives that circulate in our culture and tell us how we're supposed to behave. The *local stories* are about things like how your (or their) family fled to the U.S. from China during Mao Zedong's Cultural Revolution, your (or his) adventures at prep school, and the car accident that left you (or her) paralyzed from the waist down. The *master narratives* provide the character types and plot templates that let you locate yourself (or other people) within your society. You fall in love and configure your story according to the stock boy-meets-girl plot that structures everything from "Cinderella" to *Bridget Jones's Diary*. You help a stranger in need and she identifies you as a Good Samaritan, drawing on one of the many biblical stories that are master narratives in U.S. culture. You're good at computers and so, depending on your looks and social skills, you get typecast as either *The Matrix*'s Neo or one of the suave guys in *Revenge of the Nerds*.

Identities in the sense of the characterization question, then, are complicated narrative constructions that are generated from the first-, second-, and third-person perspectives as a way of making sense of who someone is. They come several to the customer, they're always constructed and maintained within the web of a person's social relationships, and they're often thrust upon the person rather than chosen. Some of the stories that constitute them are local and personal, whereas others connect directly to the widely shared, master narratives of the society. The backward-looking stories explain who the person has been. The forward-looking stories set the field of future action, indicating what might or must become of her.

3.2. Damaged Identities

The stories in the narrative tissue that constitutes an identity don't always do a good job of depicting the person whose identity it is, though. When the story is false and someone spreads it maliciously with the intention of discrediting you, that's slander, and if you've ever been on the receiving end of a slanderous story, you know the harm it can do. But slander isn't the only way in which identities are damaged.

There are much subtler ways, having to do with what the philosopher Diana Tietjens Meyers calls "culturally normative prejudice," and these are the ones that feminist ethicists have been most interested in.

Meyers (1994) argues that the reason prejudices spread so widely and are so hard to dislodge is that "cultures define the identities of socially excluded groups through vivid figurations that turn up in widely disseminated stories and pictures" (52)—the same stories, in fact, that I've been calling the culture's master narratives. What sustains the culturally normative prejudice against women, for example, is that supposedly factual information about gender is conveyed in imagery that captures our imagination without our ever having to think about it. Master narratives that represent women as virgins, whores, witches, and Madonnas are seductive, often absorbed unconsciously, as are images of women as babes, chicks, bitches, or dolls.

It's the unconscious absorption of these images that gives them so much of their hold over us. We take them for granted, which means we don't think about them, which means we don't have to criticize, accept, or reject them. And what often escapes us altogether is that these representations of certain groups of people aren't merely descriptive—they're *prescriptive*. They tell the members of the group how they're expected to act, and they tell everybody else how the group is supposed to be treated. "A lady never raises her voice" looks like a statement of fact, but there's a suppressed "should" in the sentence that gives it the force of a command. In just that same way, the imagery that appears to simply depict women as babes or bitches actually tells others to dismiss, control, humiliate, or hurt them.

Another reason why these images are so powerful is that evidence slides off them like water on Teflon. It doesn't matter if you've never met anyone who behaves the way the master narratives show members of that group behaving, because what the master narratives say about the group is only common sense, what everybody knows, what you don't have to think about, what's necessarily and naturally true. Evidence to the contrary—even a lot of evidence—doesn't have much power to alter what everybody knows. Things are supposed to be the way the master narratives show them to be, so if they aren't, it's the world, not the narratives, that has gotten it wrong. Worse yet, even when we *realize* that the master narrative is false, it can still exert a lot of power over us: We find ourselves reacting to the people it depicts as if it had the ultimate say over who they are.

Before we examine what kind of damage these powerful stories inflict on identities, let's consider how power constructs a society's *dominant* identities. These identities feature prominently in what might be called a social world's official story: They represent the kinds of lives that are particularly valued and visible in that world. In *Moral Passages*, for example, the philosopher Kathryn Pyne Addelson contrasts the "good girl" life plan—in which a girl is educated, dates, gets a job, is courted, marries, has sex, has children, and becomes a grandmother—with the career of the unwed mother, whose life is unplanned, interrupted, not properly under control, and not really respectable. The 'good girl' identity was dominant for much of the twentieth century, not because most girls lived it, but because planning, continuity, control, and respectability were and still are influential notions in our society.

Similarly, the identity of the white, suburban, middle-class housewife was dominant in Friedan's day, not because most women bore that identity, but because there was a widespread conviction that woman's place was in the home. The master narratives that constitute the dominant identity don't, therefore, accurately depict the social group. What they do instead is embody the ideals of those in power. Sometimes, of course, these might be very fine ideals, though they're just as apt to be silly or vicious. The more interesting point about dominant identities, though, is that the people who don't bear them often have to be, do, or ignore something so that people who are properly positioned can claim those identities (Walker 1998, 149). The Hispanic people who live in Anzaldúa's borderlands, for instance, have to speak English and ignore their own heritage, because if they didn't, the dominant white identity couldn't stay dominant.

Walker contrasts dominant identities with what she calls *necessary* identities—the ones produced by culturally normative prejudice to discredit or disempower a group that is at a social disadvantage. These identities are "necessary" in that they have to appear inevitable if they're going to conceal the coercion that holds them in place. It's much easier, for example, to keep black people out of executive boardrooms if janitorial jobs go mostly to blacks and you can point out that someone's got to clean the floors and empty the trash cans. The trick, of course, is not to let the question arise as to why it's necessary for *black* people to do those jobs. The more necessary you make it seem, the less often you will actually be called on to answer that question. The assumption that the identity is necessary takes the place of the justification that would otherwise be required for how black people are treated. Moreover, if the identity is made to seem necessary for a long enough time, the members of the group may themselves come to believe in its necessity. A few years ago the *New York Times* Sunday Magazine section ran a story about Fatma Mint Mamadou, who fled from slavery in Mauritania, where an estimated ninety thousand other human beings remain in bondage. "God created me to be a slave," Mamadou is reported to have said, "just as he created a camel to be a camel" (12 October 1997).

Necessary identities aren't merely damaged; they're what we might call "damaged to order"—damaged in respects that suit the dominant group in one way or another. They depict a subgroup as necessary insofar as they serve the dominant group's purposes, or as naturally undeserving of the dominant group's consideration, or as necessarily intolerable to the dominant group. I know a college student, living on his own for the first time, who saw a young woman of his acquaintance sewing in a shop one day and asked her to replace the buttons that had come off his shirts. It wasn't until after she told him just where he could sew those buttons that he realized he'd felt free to impose on her because he "naturally" assumed that women are supposed to look after men's personal needs. Similarly, when a judge denies a woman custody of her child on the sole grounds that she is a lesbian, he treats her as if it goes without saying that the concerns and responsibilities of lesbian mothers are unworthy of his respect. And transgendered people are regularly beaten, stripped of their jobs, or killed because they are identified as "freaks against nature" who pose an intolerable threat to dominant gender roles.

Just as some identities can be made to seem necessary, so others can be made to seem *impossible.* The philosopher of science Thomas Kuhn once pointed out how hard it is for people to identify a playing card that shows a red spade, even if they're looking straight at it. The reason is that red spades are an impossibility in the ordinary card context, so we don't expect to see them. We'd have to radically alter the way we play cards before a red spade could enter into our frame of reference. In the same way, Susan Babbitt argues, there are some identities that can't be understood, or perhaps even questioned, until existing social structures are disrupted and transformed. Ordinarily, Babbitt (1996) says, "We start with a conception of who the person is—usually defined in terms of deep-seated commitments—and define interests, responsibilities, and autonomy in these terms. In some cases, however, who a person is at a time does not provide an appropriate basis for answering such questions. In some cases, for instance, what an individual is is, in fact, degraded and dehumanized" (118–20).

Virginia Woolf makes this point quite forcefully in *A Room of One's Own,* where she imagines that Shakespeare had a wonderfully gifted sister named Judith. Unlike her brother, Judith isn't sent to school, and when her parents catch her writing plays and sonnets, they scold her for not tending to her household chores. She's married at sixteen to a wool-stapler, but driven by her genius she runs away to London, where she quickly discovers that she can't learn her craft. An apprenticeship as an actor is impossible: A woman actor is like a red spade. And even if she could teach herself how to write plays, she couldn't find the theater, the actors, and the financial backing that would allow her to put her scripts into production. Since she's barred from earning her living, she's forced to accept the protection of an actor-manager and quickly finds herself pregnant. Thwarted at every turn and unable to claim the 'playwright' identity, she kills herself in despair.

When your identity is so badly damaged that your deep-seated commitments have nowhere to go, you can't take advantage of the opportunities your society has to offer. Because your identity seems *impossible,* no doors are open to you—there is simply no place for you in your society. If, on the other hand, your identity seems *necessary*, you will also be deprived of opportunities, not because there's *no* place for you in your society, but because the place you're forced into doesn't allow you to live a full and rich life.

Deprivation of opportunity isn't the only kind of harm that's inflicted on people whose identities have been damaged by culturally normative prejudice. Many people internalize their damaged identities, thinking of themselves in the hateful or dismissive terms that their society reserves for people like them. If your consciousness is infiltrated by the degrading narratives that the dominant group contributes to your identity, you lose self-respect (or never develop it in the first place), and that too affects your ability to claim your share of the good things that are available in your society. The harm of infiltrated consciousness goes beyond the institutional barriers that your society puts in your way, because your sense of worthlessness causes you to put up your *own* barriers. In effect, you don't feel entitled to press any claims. But, like deprivation of opportunity, infiltrated consciousness occurs to greater or lesser degrees. Fatma Mint Mamadou may have been convinced that God made her a slave, but all the same she valued herself enough to run away.

3.3. Repairing the Damage

If identities consist of stories, the way to repair them is with further stories. The bigoted, morally degrading master narratives that damage the identity must be uprooted and replaced with *counterstories*—stories that resist the master narratives by portraying the subgroup more accurately and respectfully. If the identity can be fully repaired, the person whose identity it is will be able to act on the basis of it, and it will also guide other people's treatment of her. People will no longer exclude her, suppress her, force her into servitude, or dominate her, and this lets her live more freely, enjoying more opportunities and social goods.

Often, counterstories are told in two steps. The first is to notice in careful detail how the master narratives misrepresent the members of the group. The second is to clean up those misrepresentations, setting the record straight by telling a morally better story about the person or the group to which the person belongs. The counterstory's task is to correct falsehoods, so ideally it isn't itself false. It should correlate faithfully to the person's actions, since how you act says a great deal about who you are. But it also ought to provide a more comprehensive explanation of those actions than other, competing stories. That means it should try to get the proportions right, capturing the things about you that matter without minimizing them or inflating them.

Unfortunately, in an imperfect world a counterstory that meets these criteria may not be one that can be acted on. It takes time and effort for a counterstory to succeed in its aim—if it ever does—and because the master narratives that do the damage are so hard to uproot, it can be very difficult for the counterstory to be accepted by the dominant group. Consider the case of Anatole Broyard, a light-skinned black man born in New Orleans in 1920. Broyard wanted to be a writer, rather than a "Negro writer." Realizing that his work wouldn't be taken seriously if he claimed his African American identity, he did what tens of thousands of other light-skinned black Americans did, and passed as white. In the 1940s, light-skinned black men entering the military could identify themselves as "Negro" on the enlistment form and spend World War II digging latrines and cooking food for the white units, or they could check the box marked "white" and become combat soldiers, some rising in the ranks to become officers in charge of white units. Broyard checked the "white" box and never looked back. He left the service, married a white woman, and fathered two children who, even as adults, were unaware that they were part of a large black family in the South.

Broyard had the career he wanted; from the 1960s until his death in 1990 he wrote well-respected reviews and essays for the *New York Times.* Acting on the basis of a counterstory that resisted the identity of "Negro writer" was a strategy that opened doors for him and allowed him considerable freedom of action. But the counterstory was false. Rather than simply *deflating* the master narrative that attached enormous importance to his race, the story *denied* that he was black and in that way got the proportions wrong. A better counterstory, the black feminist legal theorist Anita Allen would argue, is one that preserve's African Americans' race-consciousness.

Race-consciousness, as she defines it, is "the tendency to select one's race as a subject matter of thought and conversation, but without feelings of personal inferiority" (Allen 1997, 115). Broyard's counterstory didn't let him think of himself in that way. It didn't misfire altogether, in that it freed him (if no one else) from the contemptuous treatment meted out to African Americans in a racist society, but it might have made things slightly worse for others of his race.

It's not clear, though, that any counterstory, even the most ideal one, could have done any better. Because identities are *relational,* other people have to take up the story if it's to succeed in reidentifying the members of a subgroup. As Meyers (1994) puts it, "To know who one is, one must receive recognition from others" (23). The philosopher Susan Brison also insists on the importance of recognition: It's crucial, she argues, to have other people listen empathically to your story if any kind of self-repair is to take place. Few dominant Americans in the mid-twentieth century would have been willing to listen, empathically or otherwise, to a counterstory that made it possible for Broyard's race to be a subject matter of thought and conversation, but without attributions of inferiority.

To get your counterstory heard, you have to have semantic authority—the power to make others take seriously what you have to say. That authority, though, is just what socially powerless people lack. One of the many ways in which dominant groups are privileged is that they don't have to pay attention to people in subordinate positions. Another way in which dominant groups are privileged is that they themselves do get a hearing. Taken together, these two considerations open up the possibility that a dominant group will better be able to listen to a counterstory if it's told by someone with semantic authority who speaks for those who lack it. As many feminists have pointed out, though, this is a dangerous strategy, because to speak for others can be arrogant, unethical, and politically illegitimate.

While the philosopher Linda Martín Alcoff (1995) is aware of the danger, she argues that *not* speaking for others can be just as unethical, because it leaves existing relations of dominance and subordination in place. It's a way of refusing to take responsibility for how your actions affect other people. The very fact that you can choose to speak or remain silent is itself a form of privilege that's not open to those who lack semantic authority, so if you think that by not speaking you are refusing to take advantage of your privileged status, you're kidding yourself. For that reason, Alcoff rejects the idea that privileged people should never speak for others. Instead, she proposes that people with semantic authority ask themselves four questions before they speak: (1) Do you always want to be the speaker and speak in all situations? (2) Are you leaving to those who don't share your social world all the work of translating your terms into their own and then figuring out what relevance your location has to what you're saying? (3) Are you open to criticism as a way of taking responsibility for what you say? (4) Have you thought carefully and hard about the effects on others of what you say?

In resisting and replacing the morally damaging stories that construct some people's identities according to the requirements of an abusive power system, powerless people and those who speak for them can reidentify them in ways that allow them to live more freely. But mending a damaged identity is a prolonged, messy, and morally dangerous business. It's another one of those arenas where ethics and politics can't be kept separate, where you have to start in the middle of an imperfect and actual world rather than formulate ideal theories to guide you. If any of what I've said in this chapter is true, the responsibility to be careful about what stories you contribute to your own and others' identities is a weighty one. Oddly enough, it turns out to be a matter of considerable ethical importance just who you think you are.

For Further Reading

Addelson, Kathryn Pyne. 1994. *Moral Passages: Toward a Collectivist Moral Theory.* New York: Routledge.

Alcoff, Linda Martín. 1995. "The Problem of Speaking for Others." In *Overcoming Racism and Sexism,* ed. Linda A. Bell and David Blumenfeld. Lanham, MD: Rowman & Littlefield.

Allen, Anita. 1997. "Forgetting Yourself." In *Feminists Rethink the Self,* ed. Diana Tietjens Meyers. Boulder, CO: Westview.

Babbitt, Susan M. 1996. *Impossible Dreams: Rationality, Integrity, and Moral Imagination.* Boulder, CO: Westview.

Baier, Annette. 1985. *Postures of the Mind: Essays on Mind and Morals.* Minneapolis: University of Minnesota Press.

Butler, Judith. 1990. *Gender Trouble: Feminism and the Subversion of Identity.* New York: Routledge.

Calhoun, Cheshire. 2000. *Feminism, the Family, and the Politics of the Closet: Lesbian and Gay Displacement.* New York: Oxford.

Card, Claudia. 1995. "On Race, Racism, and Ethnicity." In *Overcoming Racism and Sexism,* ed. Linda A. Bell and David Blumenfeld. Lanham, MD: Rowman & Littlefield.

Friedan, Betty. 1963. *The Feminine Mystique.* New York: W. W. Norton.

Korsgaard, Christine M. 1996. *The Sources of Normativity.* Cambridge: Cambridge University Press.

Meyers, Diana Tietjens. 1994. *Subjection and Subjectivity: Psychoanalytic Feminism and Moral Philosophy.* New York: Routledge.

Spelman, Elizabeth V. 1988. *Inessential Woman.* Boston: Beacon Press.

Walker, Margaret Urban. 1998. *Moral Understandings: A Feminist Study in Ethics.* New York: Routledge.

———. 2003. *Moral Contexts.* Lanham, MD: Rowman & Littlefield.

CHAPTER

4

Standard Moral Theories from a Feminist Perspective

When people talk of theory they can mean all kinds of things, so perhaps it would be just as well if I told you how I'm using the term here. Moral theories are formal, systematic attempts to organize our thinking about how we ought to live or what we ought to do. They seek to *explain* why certain ways of living or acting are better than others. But they also *prescribe* certain courses of conduct and provide ways of *justifying* actions, based on one account or another of what is morally valuable.

Beginning in the nineteenth century and continuing on into the twenty-first, three moral theories in particular—social contract theory, utilitarianism, and Kantian ethics—have dominated how ethics is taught and thought about in English-speaking countries. All three were originally developed between 1650 and 1800 or so, in reaction to the medieval idea that the fundamental source of morality is God and that its most authoritative teachers are the priests and pastors of the Christian church. Because these three theories emphasize rationality over religion, they are often called "Enlightenment" theories. Because the theories are associated with the rise of secular nation-states (also known as liberal democracies, since their citizens were supposed to enjoy a variety of personal freedoms), you'll hear them called "liberal" theories, as well.

Feminists have criticized the dominant liberal theories on a number of grounds, but you won't be able to decide if the criticisms are persuasive unless you have a minimal grasp of the theories themselves. We'll start with social contract theory, since that's the oldest of the three.

4.1. Social Contract Theory

Suppose there is no God to tell us what to do or punish those who disobey his commandments. And suppose too that there are no governments—no laws, no police, no courts—so that each of us can do whatever we want to. In the *Leviathan* (1651), Thomas Hobbes imagines such a "state of nature" and concludes that it would leave us badly stunted. In the state of nature, Hobbes wrote, there would be

> no place for industry, because the fruit thereof is uncertain; and consequently no culture of the earth; no navigation, nor use of the commodities that may be imported by sea; no commodious building; no instruments of moving, and removing, such things as require much force; no knowledge of the face of the earth; no account of time; no arts; no letters; no society; and which is worst of all, continual fear, and danger of violent death; and the life of man, solitary, poor, nasty, brutish, and short.

Hobbes took this dim view because outside of an ordered society, the things we need to survive are in short supply, so we would have to compete for them. And in that competition, he figured, we would look out for ourselves and maybe our families and friends, but with strangers, all bets would be off. If we were smart, we'd take what they had, even if that meant killing them. The catch is that they'd do the same to us, which is why we'd live in a state of constant fear. If this sounds too grim to be believed, think of how people behave when governments collapse, hoarding supplies, looting shops, and rioting in the streets. Or think of how often nations go to war to pursue their own interests in the absence of enforceable international laws.

The only way out of the state of nature, Hobbes thought, is for people to join forces. Peaceful coexistence is better than "the war of all against all," because then you can divide the labor that produces the goods people need, and you can distribute these goods so that everybody gets a share. Moreover, the division of labor allows you to produce *more* of everything that's necessary or useful, from food and clothing to knowledge and art. As a result, you'll be better off. But, says Hobbes, before people can coexist peacefully they must have two guarantees. The first is a guarantee that others won't harm them, and the second is a guarantee that others will stick to their agreements. You won't have much of a life if you keep having to look over your shoulder to make sure you aren't about to be stabbed in the back. And you'll be little better than a slave if you have to work for someone who promises you a weekly paycheck but keeps coming up with excuses for not living up to his end of the bargain.

The question then arises as to who or what could make these guarantees. Hobbes's answer is clear: The state. Governments can *make* the rules that are necessary if we are going to live together, and they can *enforce* these rules through the police and the courts. To escape the state of nature, then, people must agree to be governed. Hobbes believed that there really is such an agreement, and he called it the *social contract.*

The social contract, Hobbes claims, not only makes social living possible, it also makes morality possible. Under the social contract we can afford to care about others, because the contract releases us from the continual fear that previously forced us to look out only for ourselves. On the condition—and *only* on the condition—that other people will do the same thing, we can set aside our personal, self-centered inclinations in favor of obedience to the sovereign of the state. For later social contract theorists, morality consists of obeying, not the sovereign, but the set of rules that rational people would agree to follow for the benefit of all, provided that everyone else follows them too.

The most influential social contract theorist of the twentieth century is surely John Rawls, whose *Theory of Justice* (1971) offers a powerful picture of free and rational persons choosing the principles that govern the basic structure of society from behind an imaginary "veil of ignorance." The veil is hung between these people and the society they are designing, and it keeps them from seeing where they would end up in that society—what their race, sex, or social class would be, how much money they would have, or even what kind of life they would value. If they choose the principles of justice without knowing how their choice would affect them personally, Rawls argues, they won't be tempted to arrange the society in favor of their own interests. What they *will* do, he thinks, is try to maximize their share of what he calls "primary goods," the things that every rational person is presumed to want, no matter what his or her plan of life might be: "We are to suppose," says Rawls, "that each individual has a rational plan of life drawn up subject to the conditions that confront him. It schedules activities so that various desires can be fulfilled without interference." The primary goods needed for any life plan include many of the freedoms enumerated in the Bill of Rights, such as freedom of speech, freedom of conscience, freedom from arbitrary arrest, the right to own property, and the right to vote and run for office. Other primary goods are power, authority, opportunities, income, wealth, and self-respect.

So then the question is how to distribute these goods fairly. And this is where the principles of justice come in. Rawls thinks that if the people behind the veil of ignorance are rational, they will have to agree to three principles of justice, in this "lexical" order:

1. **The Liberty Principle.** Each person is to have an equal right to the most extensive system of basic liberties that's compatible with everyone else's right to the same thing. This principle is the most important, and its requirements come first.
2. **The Equality of Fair Opportunity Principle.** People with similar abilities and skills are to have equal access to offices and positions.
3. **The Difference Principle.** Inequalities in social and economic institutions are justified only if allowing them maximally benefits the people who are the worst off.

Rawls offers three justifications for these principles of justice. The first is a way of reasoning about morality he calls *reflective equilibrium*. The method ensures that our beliefs are rational, because it directs us to look at our moral principles in the light of our considered judgments in particular cases, and if there's a contradiction between the two, we are to throw out whichever one we're less sure of. Rawls thinks that our moral judgments are "considered" when we're well informed and thinking clearly, in a cool and detached manner. Let's suppose, for instance, that after collecting the facts and considering the matter dispassionately, you decide it's okay to join the Army, but at the same time, you endorse the principle that killing people is always wrong. In that case, you're contradicting yourself. One of the two beliefs has got to go, but which one you discard depends on how firmly you held them both to begin with. If joining the Army is what matters most to you, then you'll have to modify the principle against killing; if you're a committed pacifist, you'll have to find another line of work. And then you do the same thing with all the rest of your principles and considered judgments, one after the other. If you follow the method of reflective equilibrium properly, you'll end up with moral beliefs that nowhere contradict one another, and that's what makes them rational. Rawls thinks that if we put the three principles of justice into reflective equilibrium with our considered opinions about what is just or unjust in particular cases, we'll find that the principles will be consistent with those opinions.

The second justification for the three principles, says Rawls, is that they are the ones that rational people would *agree to*, voluntarily, under the ideal conditions that would obtain behind the veil of ignorance. The obligation to do what the principles require is therefore a *contractual* one. As we have seen, none of the deliberators behind the veil knows where he is going to end up in the society under construction. So if he's smart, he'll make sure that the people who are worst off get as much as they can, since he himself might be one of them. And that's what Rawls says too. According to his "maximin" argument, the rational way to choose how goods will be distributed when you don't know what *you'll* be getting is to maximize the minimal amount of primary goods that *anybody* in the society would get. You probably learned this strategy when you were a child. Maybe you and your sister had one box of Cracker Jacks between you, and your mom told you that you had to share. I'll bet she said for one of you to do the dividing and the other to have first pick. That's the maximin strategy: The one who divides doesn't know which half she'll get, so she's got a real incentive to make both halves exactly even.

The biggest complaint lodged against social contract theory is that the agreement it's based on is purely hypothetical. Nobody actually signed such a contract, and even if somebody once did, you and I certainly haven't. How, then, could it have a hold on us? Why should actual flesh-and-blood people be bound by principles of justice that were agreed on by hypothetical contractors?

Rawls's answer—and this is his third justification for the principles of justice—is borrowed from Kantian ethics: Reason commands it. Philosophical reflection, he thinks, will show us that when you and I accept the principles that fictional contractors would choose behind the veil, we express our nature as autonomous agents. Autonomy means "self-governance," and according to both Kant and Rawls, people can govern themselves because they are rational. Rationality, they argue, is the same everywhere, regardless of one's special desires or particular social position. So when we are acting as rational beings who, because we are rational, are also free to govern ourselves, we're also thinking *impartially,* not singling ourselves out for special treatment. In Rawls's version of the theory, impartial reasoning is modeled by people who enter the social contract behind the veil, where markers of race, class, gender, and so on are stripped away.

While Hobbes and Rawls are two of the most important social contract theorists, there are other versions of the theory as well. What they all have in common, though, is the concept of "morals by agreement," to use the philosopher David Gauthier's phrase. It's this ideal agreement, and the alleged rationality that underlies it, that supposedly gives morality its authority over us.

4.2. Utilitarianism

The philosophers David Hume (1711–1776), Jeremy Bentham (1748–1832), and John Stuart Mill (1806–1873) took a very different view of morality. Rather than seeing it as a matter of agreeing to rules for social conduct, they thought of it as the attempt to increase as much as possible the amount of happiness in the world. Hume originally proposed the theory, but it was Bentham who, in *The Principles of Morals and Legislation,* first formulated the Principle of Utility: The moral value of an act lies in its tendency "to augment or diminish the happiness of the party whose interest is in question." He proposed a "hedonic" (happiness) calculus for measuring this value: You add up the total happiness the act produces, subtract the pains involved, and if the benefit outweighs the burden, the act has good tendencies *on the whole*. Next you add up how many people would benefit by the act (and to what degree), subtract the number who would be harmed by it (and the degree of harm), and if more people would be helped than hurt, the act has good tendencies *for those who are affected by it*. In these calculations, everybody's happiness is to be considered impartially, "each to count as one and none for more than one." For Bentham, then, the aim of morality is to choose the action that yields the best ratio of pleasure to pain, all things considered.

Bentham's good friend was the Scottish philosopher, historian, and economist James Mill, and James's son, John Stuart Mill, was (the godless) Bentham's godson. It was John Stuart Mill who refined the theory of utilitarianism and gave it its definitive shape. In his *Utilitarianism* (1861) he formulates the Greatest Happiness Principle, according to which the ultimate end for human beings is "an existence exempt as far as possible from pain, and as rich as possible in enjoyments." Morality, Mill argues, necessarily follows this principle, bidding us to choose the course of conduct that will promote the greatest happiness for the greatest number. And since the experiences of pain and enjoyment aren't confined solely to humans, he agrees with Bentham that *all* beings capable of feeling pain are the subjects of morality. Mill distinguishes, as Bentham did not, among higher and lower pleasures, insisting that it's better to be a philosopher, however dissatisfied, than a contented pig. But he agrees with Bentham that nonhuman animals have a moral standing of their own, and their interest in not being hurt deserves equal consideration with that of human beings. "The question is not," says Bentham, "Can they *reason*? nor Can they *talk*? but, *Can they suffer?*" Most utilitarians, from Mill to the present-day Peter Singer, agree that Bentham's question is the right one.

Both Bentham and Mill took it for granted that people ought not to be interfered with except if such interference prevents harm to others. The state, they thought, should never meddle in people's lives for their own good. It's not the state's business to determine what a person's good really is, and when it tries, the result will generally be worse than if people are left to their own devices. In Mill's eloquent essay *On Liberty* (1859) he declares, "Over himself, over his own body and mind, the individual is sovereign." For that reason Mill opposed the state-sanctioned persecution of Mormons in the United States, laws punishing "victimless crimes," and state-imposed restrictions on freedom of speech.

If you take seriously the idea that you should maximize the amount of happiness in the world, you have to admit that the money you spent at the movies last night should have gone to Oxfam or some other organization that feeds starving people in war-torn nations, since saving their lives is surely more important than your frivolous pleasures. You'd obviously have to scale back your standard of living, and instead of going out to the bars with your friends, you'd need to volunteer at the homeless shelter and probably the animal shelter as well. But where do you draw the line? Do you have to give up your college education and turn over your tuition money to the poor? Do you have to renounce your cushy job and start building houses for the homeless? It seems as if the unlimited demands of utilitarianism elbow out most of the things that give meaning to our lives, including (as the philosopher Bernard Williams complains) any reason we might have to take morality seriously. Moreover, not only does utilitarianism seem to leave no room for our personal plans and projects, it also seems to give you no time for special attention to friends and family, because it insists that we figure out the consequences for everyone equally, no matter how they are related to us. And finally, the demand that we calculate precisely the burdens and benefits of our acts grotesquely violates our commonsense belief that moral value can't be assigned by crunching numbers.

In *The Methods of Ethics* (1874) the utilitarian Henry Sidgwick introduces the "indirect strategy" for getting around these objections. He argues that while maximizing happiness is the proper *standard* for judging actions, it's not the only or always the best *motive* for acting. If a father takes care of his baby because he loves him, utilitarianism doesn't require him to stop and think whether his action promotes the general happiness. A painter can paint because she needs to, not because her pictures make others happy. You can have dinner with your friend because you like him, not because dining with friends makes the world a better place. But the moral worth of these acts can be *assessed* by thinking about how unhappy we'd be if there were no love, art, or friendship in the world.

Besides, as Mill and Sidgwick both point out, utilitarian moral theory isn't meant for ordinary people in ordinary circumstances. "The occasions," says Mill, "on which any person (except one in a thousand) has it in his power . . . to be a public benefactor, are but exceptional; and on these occasions alone is he called on to consider public utility; in every other case, private utility, the interest or happiness of some few persons, is all he has to attend to." Sidgwick puts the point even more bluntly, remarking that it may be best, on utilitarian grounds, for ordinary people not to be utilitarians at all. It's better for them to believe that the morality they're already familiar with is "absolutely and universally prescribed, since any other view of it may dangerously weaken its hold over their minds." Utilitarianism, he thinks, is a moral theory for the exceptional—"either for persons generally under exceptional circumstances, or for a class of persons defined by exceptional qualities of intellect, temperament, or character."

Not all utilitarians are quite so plainspoken. Nor do they all aim at maximizing pleasure or happiness. Some utilitarians think it's more important to satisfy as many *preferences* as possible, while others think the best thing is to meet the greatest number of *interests.* And many utilitarians focus on *rules* for acting, rather than single actions. What they all agree on, though, is that acts (or rules) are to be judged right or wrong solely on the basis of their *consequences* for all affected parties, with no one singled out for special consideration.

4.3. Kantian Ethics

The consequences be damned, says Immanuel Kant (1724–1804). In the *Groundwork of the Metaphysic of Morals* (1785), he argues that consequences have nothing whatsoever to do with the morality of an action. For Kant the point of morality is freedom; the main problem is how to achieve it; and the solution, which reason commands, is to be a law-giving citizen in a "kingdom" of other free lawgivers.

To act freely, Kant says, is to act without being constrained either by other people or by the laws of nature. If there's a gun to your head you can't act freely, and if you have to do what your genetic makeup forces you to do (think of how pigeons behave), you aren't free either. Although Kant thinks we can't know for sure that we are free, the fact that we're rational gives us good grounds for supposing we are. To understand what he means, all you have to do is think about what's motivating you when you fill in the last line of this ancient argument:

All men are mortal.

Socrates is a man.

Therefore ________________________.

When you say to yourself, "Therefore Socrates is mortal," it doesn't seem as if you're obeying any law of biology, like the reflex that dilates your pupils when you move from sunlight into the dark. And you surely aren't obeying any law of physics, like the one you have to comply with if you fall out of a second-story window. Whatever it is that lets you make the inference about Socrates' mortality, it seems to have nothing to do with the laws governing the natural world. And not having to obey the dictates of nature is a kind of negative freedom.

But independence from natural forces isn't really freedom, says Kant, if it's lawless. Freedom, after all, isn't the same as anarchy, and free people aren't just loose cannons, plowing into things on a whim or acting out of perversity. If you're free you act for *reasons,* and reasons, Kant thinks, must be based on some principle. Let's suppose your principle for acting is this one: "Always do what your parents tell you." If you adopt this principle, are you acting freely? No, because you've put yourself under your parents' law. And if your principle is "Do whatever makes you feel good," you aren't free either, because then you've made yourself a slave to your own appetites. Kant thinks there's only one principle that lets you be free, and that's the one that has no constraint on it of any kind except that it gives law.

What makes something a law is that its scope is universal. "Sally should pay George next Tuesday" is *not* a law, because it applies only to Sally. Universalize it as "People should pay back their debts" and it *is* a law, binding not only on Sally but on everybody else as well. Law is impartial, applying to everyone and favoring no one. "People should pay their debts," though, isn't the law that lets us be free, because it has a specific content and that constrains it so that the *content,* rather than we ourselves, ends up telling us what to do. The law we're looking for preserves our autonomy by letting *us* choose what we're going to do. It has no content at all. It's merely the form of law.

And what is this law that has no content but only form? I already gave you a hint when I said that what makes something a law is that its scope is universal. The law that's all form and no content is the law that says, "Universalize!" Or, if you prefer, "Apply your reason for acting to everybody!" Nobody can make us obey this law, because we're free. And we can *remain* free, says Kant, only if we obey it. If we don't, either other people or our own passions will govern us. This law (usually translated as an "imperative") binds us categorically. That is, there are no "ands" or "ifs" about it. A hypothetical imperative, by contrast, is one you ought to follow *if* you care about achieving a certain goal: *If* you want to avoid sexually transmitted disease, you ought to use a condom. *If* you want to lose weight, you ought to get more exercise. Hypothetical imperatives are possible, says Kant, because we have desires. The Categorical Imperative, on the other hand, is possible because we have the ability to reason. It binds us simply because, Kant thinks, every rational person must accept it.

The Categorical Imperative (which Kant also calls the Supreme Principle of Morality) is formulated three different ways in the *Groundwork.* The first formulation, which emphasizes the idea that the law is all form and no content, is this one: **Act only on that maxim through which you can at the same time will that it should become a universal law.** By "maxim," Kant means your reason for acting. What he's telling you here is that if, say, your reason for running a red light is that you're in a hurry, you should ask yourself whether "People should always run red lights when they're in a hurry" is a law that everybody could act on without contradiction. Kant thinks that if you asked yourself this question, you'd see that you're trying to have it both ways: You want the law against running red lights to be a law for everybody, but not be a law for you. Since nothing can be a law and not be a law at the same time, you're caught in a contradiction. And as contradictions are irrational, your own ability to reason will show you that you can't act on this maxim.

Because people's ability to reason makes them so valuable you can't set a price on them (their humanity gives them "dignity" rather than price), the second formulation goes like this: **Act in such a way that you always treat humanity, whether in your own person or in the person of any other, never simply as a means, but always at the same time as an end.** Note that Kant does *not* say that you must never treat people as means to your ends. When you order a pizza, you're using the delivery person as a means to your end and there's certainly nothing wrong with that (at least, not if you remember to tip). What the second formulation forbids is your using other people as if they didn't have their own purposes and desires—as if the only reason for their existence was to serve you. While it sounds odd to talk about using the humanity in your *own* person merely as means to your ends, I think what Kant has in mind is a case where a person's reason tells her she can't have something she wants, so she throws reason out the window and goes for that thing all the same. Dismissing your ability to reason when it gets in your way is deeply disrespectful of yourself, because it's your ability to reason, Kant thinks, that makes you so precious. This formulation of the Categorical Imperative underscores the idea that your worth isn't just instrumental—you're valuable for yourself alone, not merely because you're useful.

And all other people are valuable in and of themselves too, just like you. That's the idea of the third formulation: **All maxims as proceeding from our own making of law ought to harmonize with a possible kingdom of ends as a kingdom of nature.** Because the laws you make for yourself, by an act of your own autonomy, must be laws for all other free lawmakers as well, you have to be sure that your laws don't contradict theirs. This formulation seems to be a restatement of the first, in that it commands you to universalize whatever reasons you have for acting so that they are reasons for everyone. But the picture here is of a *kingdom* of self-legislators—a kingdom in which every citizen is king. It's a beautiful picture if you stop to think about it: a free people, living together as self-legislating citizens in a kingdom where, because they are rational, they're free. And because the rationality that produces their freedom also gives them a worth that's "unconditioned and incomparable," as Kant puts it, they honor the goodness of others as well as their own.

The Categorical Imperative is particularly useful for stopping people from treating themselves as exceptions to the rule. But as some philosophers see it, that's just the problem. A major objection to the whole Kantian line of thought is that it's hard to make sense of the idea that moral rules allow no exceptions. Is it really true, for example, that you must *never* run a red light when you're in a hurry, even to take a woman in labor to a hospital in the middle of the night when there's no other car anywhere near the intersection?

And what are you supposed to do when you have two rules, each of which forbids something unconditionally, and the only choice that lies before you is to do one or the other of them? It's not hard to come up with an example of this kind of clash between absolutes. Let's say that the Categorical Imperative shows you that you must never take someone else's property without his or her permission, because if you make a law that other people must keep their hands off your things but it's not a law for you, you generate a contradiction. And let's say too that the Categorical Imperative shows you that you must always keep morally permissible promises, again because you can make yourself an exception to this law only on pain of contradiction. Now suppose that since you're a natural slob, your brother made you promise you'd be properly dressed at his wedding. When you get to the church, though, you suddenly notice a big stain on your tie. The service is about to begin and there's nobody left in the vestry, but the minister has left a tie hanging on the back of the door. To obey the law about not breaking promises, you'll have to take someone else's property. To obey the law about not taking other people's property, you'll have to break a promise. But if Kant is right and moral rules are unconditional, you are categorically forbidden to do either of these things, even though they're the only two options open to you. How on earth does *that* make sense?

It's a puzzle, all right, and we have Kant's deepest sympathy. In the final paragraph of the *Groundwork* he says, "It is no discredit to our deduction of the supreme principle of morality, but rather a reproach which must be brought against reason as such, that it cannot make comprehensible the absolute necessity of an unconditioned practical law. . . . While we do not comprehend the practical unconditioned necessity of the moral imperative, we do comprehend its *incomprehensibility*." Philosophy can take you only so far, Kant suggests. The rest is silence.

4.4. What's Wrong with This Picture?

These thumbnail sketches of the most prominent moral theories are meant to give you an idea of the differences among them, which are surely considerable. Less visible, perhaps, is how much the theories have in common. But it's their commonalities that trouble many feminists, so rather than offer criticisms of each theory in turn, I'll show you three pictures that underlie all of them and explain what it is that feminists think the pictures get wrong. These pictures are simplifications, of course. And what they portray emerges only if you stand back and notice the things the theories emphasize, the things they take for granted, and the things they don't mention. When you do that you start to see, first, the picture of the person who is supposed to act on the theories; second, the picture of the society in which this person lives; and third, the picture of human reason that the person exercises when making moral judgments. Let's examine these pictures with an awareness of how power operates in the guise of gender, so that we can see more clearly what they distort, paint over, or leave out altogether. (This is an instance of Lindemann's ad hoc rule Number 37: When the Wizard of Oz says, "Pay no attention to the man behind the screen," be sure to take a closer look.)

The Picture of the Person

The first thing to notice about the people who are meant to lead their lives in accordance with the theories is that they are detached from other people. They act on their own, unconstrained by their relationships to family or friends. They might *have* such relationships, but the theories aren't much interested in them. Hobbes populates the State of Nature with individuals who spring up out of the ground full grown, like mushrooms. The citizens of the Kingdom of Ends don't seem to have had parents either, not to mention lovers or children. And if utilitarian moral agents have special responsibilities to housemates, siblings, or grandparents, you won't find that out by reading Mill. None of the theories does much to ensure that people will have any connections to one another aside from the minimal ones needed to keep the society from collapsing, and all of them picture the agent as what the philosopher Charles Taylor calls a "punctual self"—a dot on a page, unconnected to other dots.

The second thing to notice is that these people are self-sufficient. You can tell this because they all want to be let alone. Hobbes isn't worried about what would happen if he became ill—he's worried that his neighbors will attack him. The Categorical Imperative operates primarily to tell you what you *mustn't do to* other people, not what you *should do for* them. Mill is worried more about state interference in people's lives than about the ways the state might be able to give aid to the needy. For the most part, the theories take it for granted that the people they are talking about can look after themselves without any help from anybody.

The third thing to notice is that each of these people has just as much social power as everyone else. None of them is socially disadvantaged and none has to report to a higher-up. The parties to the social contract are presumed to negotiate from positions of equality, and indeed in the Rawlsian version of the theory, this presumption is explicitly built in. Kantian persons are lawgivers and judges, powerful enough so they don't have to notice that the laws they'd be willing to accept might not be equally acceptable to socially disadvantaged people for whom the laws could be harmful or beside the point. And utilitarian persons don't have to report to any higher-up because they *are* the higher-ups. As Sidgwick so revealingly put it, utilitarianism is for "a class of persons defined by exceptional qualities of intellect, temperament, or character," who by virtue of these qualities are fitted to make policies for the public good. Williams calls these people "government house" utilitarians, because it's easy to imagine them as bureaucrats, government officials, or corporate managers.

The fourth thing to notice is that the people are calculators and planners. The individuals who are hammering out the social contract are trying in a self-interested fashion to get the best bargain they can for themselves, which requires a certain amount of gamesmanship—knowledge of the maximin strategy, for example—as each determines his own advantage by figuring out what other people are likely to do. Rawlsian social contractors all have rational life plans: They know where they're going in the long run, and they exercise the watchful self-control that's required to get them there. Bentham's and Mill's moral agents are rational planners too, though as managers and policy makers, they typically direct their planning toward others rather than themselves. And Kantian moral agents are the quintessential calculators: What's morally valuable about them—and the *only* source of their value—is their ability to reason.

The trouble with the picture of the persons who populate these theories—the judge, the policy maker, the manager, the contractor, the gamesman—is that it represents, in ideal form, the responsibilities, privileges, and concerns of only *some* actual people in a certain kind of society and, even then, only at a particular time in their lives. The kind of person who is supposed to act on these theories is both unattached and self-sufficient; he's the powerful equal of the other people to whom the theory applies; he promotes his own interests or the interests of those he's responsible for and assumes his peers will do the same; he enters freely into contracts with other free contractors; he uses his reason to plan out the course of his own life or to manage and coordinate the efforts of others; and he commands the resources needed to do these things.

What a number of you will find missing from these accounts is large chunks of your own experience of life. Indeed, what many of you won't find there is *yourselves*. Though the theories don't acknowledge it, the picture of the ideal or representative person they offer is, as Margaret Urban Walker (1998) aptly puts it, "none of us at all times, and many of us at no times" (21–22). In particular, the idealized picture of independent, powerful agents seeking to promote their own interests, plan for themselves and others, or enhance their autonomy through voluntary and impersonal interactions misrepresents many *women's* lives. Which people get to live the kind of life these theories depict depends on their gender, race, age, class, and the other factors on which the uneven distribution of social privilege is based. And this is a problem for three different reasons.

First of all, it's a problem because, as a representation of what real people are really like, it's false. None of us stands on our own; we all live firmly embedded within a thick web of social relationships. We couldn't even *be* the persons we are if it weren't for all the other persons who respond to us, care for us, teach us, include us in their activities, and find room for us in their society. This is what Annette Baier means when she says we are all "second persons," persons produced by other persons rather than punctual selves. Moreover, all of us have needed help at various points in our lives and will doubtless need it again. Then too, many people aren't in a position to pursue their own interests by bargaining on equal terms with other contractors—to quote Baier (1994) again, "Contract is a device for traders, entrepreneurs, and capitalists, not for children, servants, indentured wives, and slaves" (113). Many people have to follow policies made by others, rather than make policy themselves. And the circumstances of many people's lives don't permit them to make long-range plans, while other people don't think it's very important to live their lives according to a long-range plan.

Second, if the picture of persons underlying these theories isn't supposed to represent real people but instead is meant to be an ideal toward which all real people ought to strive, then it's still false, because it's impossible. If you're going to get anywhere near the ideal yourself, you need vast amounts of support from other people who, because they're supporting you, can't have the kind of life you live. Who is supposed to nurture, protect, and socialize children so that they can grow up to be self-sufficient utilitarians? Who is supposed to take care of autonomous individuals when they fall ill or are badly injured? Who is supposed to do the social contractors' laundry, clean their bathrooms, or cook their meals so that they are free to pursue their life plans? To realize the ideal you need people—mostly, they've been women—to look after you, but because they're looking after you, they aren't free to realize the ideal for themselves.

Third, the idealized representation of persons on which these theories are based isn't just false, it's harmful. Though all of us are supposed to aim at it, the ideal isn't necessarily the best or only one. Some people—those suffering from Alzheimer's dementia or mentally retarded people, for example—couldn't possibly hope to be autonomous in the sense that Kant means, but they might have very good lives if they (and the rest of us) aimed at something else. Other people have excellent reasons to reject various aspects of the ideal on moral, political, religious, or personal grounds. But because the standard theories are dominant in our culture, the actual people who can't or don't conform to their picture of the ideal person appear substandard or morally defective, not what "we" are or should be. When people appear to be morally defective, they are often treated as morally defective, and this restricts their ability to live responsibly and well.

The Picture of Society

The second picture on which these prominent moral theories are based is that of a society consisting of two spheres: the public and the private. The public sphere is the one in which people's freedom is secured by rights. These rights are couched negatively, in terms of things the state or other individuals may not do to you, and can fairly be summed up as the right not to be interfered with. Because freedom is the central value of this sphere, it is governed by a "thin" conception of the good life—that is, the view of what it means to live well is left deliberately sketchy so that each person can decide for himself what's important in life and how best to achieve it. The public sphere is therefore the sphere in which people make choices. The public sphere is also the place for impartiality: No one's interests or rights are to count for more than anyone else's. And finally, in the public sphere the laws or principles for conduct are universal and impersonal. The supposedly impersonal and universal nature of truth itself gives these laws their authority.

If the public sphere is the sphere of rights, the private sphere is the sphere of the good. It's here that people pursue their various "thick" visions of the best way to live, whether as a practicing Catholic, a housewife, a fraternity brother, or whatever. The private sphere is the one in which relationships and the responsibilities that arise from them are frequently unchosen. It's the place for favoritism, because it's the sphere of friendship, love, and families—relationships in which another person is singled out for special consideration rather than treated like everybody else. The private sphere is particularistic rather than universal; it's quirky, unsystematic, and personal.

Any theory that is primarily concerned with the basic structure of society, or says each person is to count for one and none for more than one, or tells you that if you do something for one person you have to be willing to do it for all, is focusing on relationships in the public sphere, not the private. For that reason it's sometimes said that the dominant theories treat the private sphere as if it isn't the business of morality. This isn't strictly true, of course. None of the theories permits you to kill your girlfriend as long as you do it in the privacy of your own home, for example. But all three theories fail utterly to acknowledge the morally crucial labor that must be done in families and other private places if society is to function at all. It's in the places marked "private" that vast amounts of unpaid and socially unrecognized work goes on—the work of forming and maintaining selves, caring for children and others who need it, and transmitting morality from one generation to the next. And because this work is *gendered,* in that it's primarily women who are expected to do it, the theories in effect withhold moral recognition from many of the activities that make up most women's lives.

Because the dominant moral theories offer a picture of the public sphere as one in which each person is just as free as every other, they represent women as having choices about whether to engage in the reproductive labor of the private sphere. The theories show women choosing to provide loving maternal care, or persuading their husbands to provide loving paternal care, or deciding to have an abortion. But here again the picture is false. Many women don't have these choices: The fathers of their children walk out on them; they have no access to abortion or their moral beliefs forbid it; the child is a niece or granddaughter with nobody else to look after her. Even if reproductive choices really *were* optional, though, it could still be objected that no decent moral theory leaves the care of new or future children solely up to those who choose to provide it.

Although social contract theory, utilitarianism, and Kantian ethics offer a picture of society whose public sphere is supposed to be governed by impartiality and universality, this too is false. As the picture of the persons who inhabit this society has already shown us, the theories are not impartial. Instead, they favor persons whose social standing, concerns, and occupations look suspiciously like those of well-to-do white men. The ideal of impartiality is intended to emphasize the ways in which we're all alike, which is why the theories assume that in the public sphere, people's basic interests are the same. They assume, for example, that while we all might have different plans for how to get ahead in our jobs, we all basically care about living according to plan. But even in the workplace or marketplace, not all people basically care about living according to plan, or about not being interfered with, or about bargaining on equal terms with others. The assumption that they do tends to steamroll over the differences in people's needs, their cultural traditions, and how they're expected to act when they're in public.

Nor are the theories in fact universal, because they center on relations among independent strangers in the male-dominated public world of work and politics. Those relations are important only to certain sorts of people, and they're out of the question or a matter of indifference to many others. If the theories were truly concerned with including as many people as possible, wouldn't they focus instead on the lack of control, the dependency, and the relations of love and friendship that make up the fabric of most people's everyday lives?

Attention to these matters would quickly reveal the importance of the particular and the personal in all of morality, not just the part that's supposed to govern the public sphere. A great many of the choices we make in our everyday lives can't and shouldn't be universalized. I may not be aiming at the same things you are striving for; I might not want or need to go where you do. The notion of universality effectively excludes people who look (suspiciously) like women and men of color from the society the liberal theories depict. By carving that society into two spheres and populating the private sphere with anybody who doesn't fit the "universal" norm, the theories keep such people from participating fully in the social contract, pure Kantian rationality, or the promotion of the public good.

All of which is to say that the division of society into two spheres is a fiction. It serves the social contract, Kantian, and utilitarian theories well, because it creates a boundary that can be policed so that the preoccupations of powerful people in a certain kind of society are seen as the important ones—the ones that are governed by morality. The reality, however, is that morality can't be boxed off in this way. It permeates all of society, including the parts where the misfits live.

The Picture of Rationality

What gives morality its hold over us? Why, that is, should we do the right thing if it's inconvenient or embarrassing or even costs us our life? One possible answer is "Because God commands it," but that answer doesn't satisfy people who (a) don't believe in God or (b) believe in God but aren't sure we know precisely what he wants us to do ("Thou shalt not kill." Not even in self-defense? In war? How about animals?). The dominant theories, rejecting religious faith as the basis for morality, tell us we have to do the right thing because *reason* commands it. Now, reason is a fine thing. Feminist moral theorists are delighted when people offer reasons for what they do and tackle their moral disagreements with other people in a rational manner. But they aren't altogether happy with the picture of rationality that underlies social contract, Kantian, and utilitarian theories.

For one thing, the picture leaves a lot out. It excludes the emotions, rather than acknowledging that feelings such as empathy, resentment, or anger play a useful role in our moral thinking. It excludes what we care about, rather than acknowledging that what we care about often *is* the reason we ought to do something. It excludes trust, rather than acknowledging that trust is what keeps our moral judgments from being paranoid. And it excludes narrative or other representational modes of reasoning, rather than acknowledging that stories and images are powerful tools for making moral sense of the world and our place in it.

Furthermore, the picture exaggerates the role of reason in morality. The method of reasoning recommended by Rawls, for example, is that you put your considered moral judgments into reflective equilibrium with your moral principles so that none of your beliefs contradict any other. But suppose you were raised to believe that the white race is superior to all other races, and when you grew up, having never interacted with people who weren't white, you thought it over carefully and concluded that whites really *are* superior, with the result that you now hold the belief very firmly. And suppose all of your moral principles are consistent with this belief. In that case, your system of beliefs is in reflective equilibrium, so it's rational. The trouble is, it's also *evil.* Even if you follow the method very carefully, you can't count on it to rid you of bigotry and prejudice.

And finally, the picture shows reason operating at high levels of abstract idealization, which tends to produce bad arguments. Consider this one, from the philosopher Christine Korsgaard's *Sources of Normativity* (1996, 143). Korsgaard imagines that you are tormenting a stranger and he calls on you to stop, asking how you would like it if someone did the same to you. Unless you take the stranger's words as mere noise, she says, you are acknowledging that this is a human being speaking. Then, like the good Kantian philosopher she is, she argues that since you see *yourself* as worthy of moral consideration "in so far as you are just human, just *someone,*" your rationality compels you to see that the stranger's humanity deserves moral consideration as well. If you don't, she concludes, you're being inconsistent. But as Walker points out in *Moral Contexts* (143–45), this argument assumes that you think the stranger is just like you in being human, and you're just like him in being human. In many cases, though, people *don't* think that others are just human beings exactly like themselves. They think there are different *kinds* of human beings and that some kinds may be enslaved, others may be slaughtered, still others may be outlawed, and others yet again are fit only to satisfy the sexual and domestic wants of men. If you think there are different kinds of human beings, then you *aren't* being inconsistent in doing to a stranger what you wouldn't want done to you. We can deplore the fact that many people do think certain kinds of people are fair game for abusive treatment, but the problem isn't that they're irrational. They only look that way if rationality is idealized and abstracted from the social and moral contexts in which actual people live.

4.5. The PowerPoint Problem

Taken together, then, the three pictures underlying social contract theory, utilitarianism, and Kantian ethics suggest that the theories really aren't up to the job of illuminating the moral experience of all people, everywhere. In particular, they are silent about a number of the activities, concerns, and circumstances that make up the greater part of the lives of many women and many men of color, especially if they are poor, disabled, gay, old, or otherwise disadvantaged by their social situation.

Well, *could* the theories speak to the moral situation of the people they have neglected? Do these silences imply in a strictly logical way that the theories can't handle the moral realities of socially disadvantaged people? No. I suspect that in fact they can't, but my talk of pictures is deliberate, because pictures don't logically imply anything—they represent a state of affairs. It's the actual state of affairs that's important here, not what might in principle be possible. The question isn't whether the theories *couldn't* accommodate the experience of women and relatively powerless men; the point is that they don't. Their repeated, intensive focus on certain topics in moral theorizing and their consistent exclusion of others has created what Cheshire Calhoun calls an "ideology of the moral life." It's an ideology because it's politically loaded in favor of privileged white men and because it represents as natural and normal what is actually the effect of social power. As a direct result of what it emphasizes and what it leaves out, certain kinds of moral capacities and knowledge, important differences among people, and the moral demands that make up the bulk of many people's day-to-day lives don't get registered as the proper concerns of a moral theory at all. The ideology keeps forcing our attention back on the topics and problems that matter to the ideal man who is supposed to, but doesn't, symbolize all of us.

You could think of this as the PowerPoint problem. If you've ever put together a PowerPoint presentation, you know that while the software offers you a number of content layouts, text-and-content layouts, and text-and-graph layouts, it offers only two standardized text layouts: a page-width layout with a title and bullet-points, and a two-column layout with a title and bullet-points. The page-width layout lets you display a string of facts with supporting points under each, and the two-column layout lets you compare or contrast two items. That's it. If you want to compare three items, you're out of luck, and if you want to circle around an idea instead of laying it out in a linear fashion, you can't do that either. Nor can you present a conversation or a story. If you're very clever you might be able to customize the layout, but there's no easy way to do it, so the chances are you won't. As a result, you are repeatedly forced into a very limited kind of thinking—the kind that's used by the corporate executives for which the software program seems to have been designed. And because PowerPoint is the dominant technology for making presentations, the more you use it, the more likely it is that you'll consider that kind of thinking normal and right.

I believe that the three most widely known moral theories are plagued by a feminist version of the PowerPoint problem. As Baier (1994) puts it, "The great moral theorists in our tradition not only are all men, [but] with a few significant exceptions . . . they are a collection of clerics, misogynists, and puritan bachelors" (3). The theories reflect their authors' social circumstances, focusing on the sorts of preoccupations and concerns that mark a certain kind of prosperous and respectable masculine life. And because they are *dominant* theories, they offer no incentive to take account of other kinds of lives: If you study them long enough, you'll consider that way of doing ethics normal and right.

Is there any point, then, in studying Kant and Mill and Rawls? Of course there is. In the first place, the dominant theorists should be studied just because they *are* dominant. They've provided a vocabulary and a set of ideas that help us to make moral sense of each other. The second reason to study them is that many of the concepts, arguments, distinctions, and methodologies they have developed are well worth having: They help us sort out what we ought to do and why we ought to do it. These theorists are powerful voices in a long-standing conversation in Western culture about crucially important questions concerning human existence: How might we best live together? Who should I strive to be? What should I care about? What must I take responsibility for? All morally developed persons must find their own answers to questions of this kind, but they don't have to do it all by themselves. There are rich resources at their disposal in the standing theories.

While the theories can't be dismissed, then, their neglect of gender and other factors that determine who has power over whom means that those of us who want to think clearly and carefully about ethics have got our work cut out for us. We have to get a better understanding of the consequences for ethics of taking seriously the moral claims and perspectives of people who don't occupy positions of social privilege. What happens when moral theory becomes skeptical of ideal relationships of equality as the basis for morality and shifts its focus to relationships of dependency and vulnerability? What happens when moral selves are represented as having bodies and emotions as well as minds? What happens when ethical attention moves from an idealized, supposedly universal human nature to particular persons and social groups? I'll take up these questions in the next chapter.

For Further Reading

Baier, Annette C. 1985. "Cartesian Persons." In *Postures of the Mind: Essays on Mind and Morals*. Minneapolis: University of Minnesota Press.

———. 1994. *Moral Prejudices: Essays on Ethics*. Cambridge, MA: Harvard University Press.

Calhoun, Cheshire. 1988. "Justice, Care, Gender Bias." *Journal of Philosophy* 85 (9): 451–63.

Code, Lorraine. 1987. "Second Persons." In *Science, Morality, and Feminist Theory,* ed. Marsha Hanen and Kai Nielsen. Calgary: University of Calgary Press.

Held, Virginia. 1987. "Non-contractual Society: A Feminist View." In *Science, Morality, and Feminist Theory,* ed. Marsha Hanen and Kai Nielsen. Calgary: University of Calgary Press.

Korsgaard, Christine M. 1996. *The Sources of Normativity.* Cambridge: Cambridge University Press.

Rawls, John. 1971. *A Theory of Justice.* Cambridge, MA: Harvard University Press.

Walker, Margaret Urban. 1998. *Moral Understandings: A Feminist Study in Ethics.* New York: Routledge.

———. 2003. *Moral Contexts.* Lanham, MD: Rowman & Littlefield.

CHAPTER

5

Feminist Ethics of Care and Responsibility

The late Harvard psychologist Lawrence Kohlberg claimed that people become morally mature by going through certain distinct stages. You, being a mature adult, have presumably outgrown the idea that being good means helping and pleasing other people (stage 3 on Kohlberg's scale), and you've come to see that morality consists of a set of rules for maintaining the social order (stage 4). You might even be mature enough to sum up the rules in a principle such as "the greatest good for the greatest number" (stage 5) or to think of morality in terms of self-chosen universal principles of justice (stage 6), though Kohlberg claimed that not everyone reaches these heights of maturity.

To determine where you are on Kohlberg's scale, you could think about this dilemma, which is one in the series he created to measure moral development in adolescence:

> In Europe, a woman was near death from cancer. One drug might save her, a form of radium that a druggist in the same town had recently discovered. The druggist was charging $2,000, ten times what the drug cost him to make. The sick woman's husband, Heinz, went to everyone he knew to borrow the money, but he could only get together about half of what it cost. He told the druggist that his wife was dying and asked him to sell it cheaper or let him pay later. But the druggist said, "No." The husband got desperate and broke in to the man's store to steal the drug for his wife. Should the husband have done that? Why?

Because your level of moral maturity has presumably hit stage 4 or higher, you're old enough to think about Heinz's dilemma in terms of conflicting rules: There's the rule about saving lives, but there's also the rule against stealing. So, if you tackle the dilemma the way Kohlberg thought you would, you'll weigh these rules against each other. Since the rule that says "save life" takes priority over the rule that says "don't steal," you'll conclude that Heinz was justified in stealing the drug.

Kohlberg, heavily influenced by the impartial, impersonal, universalistic theories of morality we've just explored, and convinced that Kantian ethics was superior to utilitarianism, thought that the moral reasoning of mature adults must conform to one or the other of the dominant theories. But when Carol Gilligan, another Harvard psychologist, conducted her own studies of moral development, she heard many of her research subjects speaking to her "in a different voice." Rather than talking about rights and rules, they were using the language of relationships and connection. Rather than abstract reasoning, their thinking was contextual and concrete. And, Gilligan argued, this "different voice" was especially likely to be heard when the research subjects were girls and women. Note the contrast, for example, between eleven-year-old Jake's way of thinking about Heinz's dilemma and how eleven-year-old Amy tackles it.

> JAKE: For one thing, a human life is worth more than money, and if the druggist only makes $1,000, he is still going to live, but if Heinz doesn't steal the drug, his wife is going to die. *(Why is life worth more than money?)* Because the druggist can get a thousand dollars later from rich people with cancer, but Heinz can't get his wife again. *(Why not?)* Because people are all different and so you couldn't get Heinz's wife again.

Jake, who thinks "the only thing that is totally logical" is math, considers the moral dilemma to be "sort of like a math problem with humans."

> AMY: *(Should Heinz steal the drug?)* Well, I don't think so. I think there might be other ways besides stealing it, like if he could borrow the money or make a loan or something, but he really shouldn't steal the drug—but his wife shouldn't die either. *(Why shouldn't he steal the drug?)* If he stole the drug, he might save his wife then, but if he did, he might have to go to jail, and then his

> wife might get sicker again, and he couldn't get more of the drug, and it might not be good. So, they should really just talk it out and find some other way to make the money.

Amy, who sees the problem as a narrative of relationships that extend over time instead of taking Jake's "freeze frame" view of it, is concerned to maintain rather than break off connections: "The world should just share things more and then people wouldn't have to steal" (Gilligan 1982, 26–29).

According to Kohlberg's measurements, Jake is a stage 4 thinker, while Amy clearly is still at stage 3. But is Amy really morally less mature than Jake? Gilligan doesn't think so. Instead, she explains the difference between the two as a difference in moral orientation: Jake is oriented toward what she calls "justice," while Amy is oriented toward "care." Girls and women tend to look immature on Kohlberg's scale, says Gilligan, because Kohlberg based his findings on a study of 84 boys whose development he followed for a period of 20 years, and in that study, the justice orientation predominates. Gilligan is careful to say that the "different voice" is *not* the voice of all women, across cultures and through time, any more than the voice of justice is the voice of all men. Even so, in a society like ours, "social status and power combine with reproductive biology to shape the experience of males and females and the relations between the sexes," and this gendered experience produces "different modes of moral understanding" (Gilligan 1982, 2, 32). The mode that's concerned with the activity of care centers morality around the understanding of responsibility and relationships, while the mode that's concerned with justice centers morality around the understanding of rights and rules.

Notice the connection Gilligan draws between what people experience and how they think. The people who lived through the Great Depression of the 1930s, for instance, tended to hoard and save even when times were good again. Similarly, people who've lived on their own for a long time tend to be a little self-absorbed. But it's not only experiences of this kind that shape our thinking. As the philosopher Sara Ruddick (1989) explains, thinking also "arises from and is shaped by the practices in which people engage" (9). A practice is a socially recognized, regular way of doing something that has a point to it. Basketball is a practice: There are rules for how you play it and the point is to score more baskets than the opposing team. Farming is a very different kind of practice, but it too has rules for doing it properly and its point is to produce food and fibers. Education is a practice; so is law; so is e-mailing.

Although the moral theories we've been looking at have had little to say about this, some practices get more respect than others, and the knowledge connected with those practices carries a certain authority. There will be times when you'd much rather have, say, a plumber's knowledge than a lawyer's, but when the bathroom's mopped up and the toilet is working again, you'll find it easy to agree that a lawyer's knowledge is socially more authoritative than is the plumber's. Whose knowledge actually counts as knowledge, and who gets to say what counts, are functions, in part, of how power is distributed within a society. Those who are "in a position to know" are the people who participate in the practices—medicine, science, law, politics, higher education, corporate management—that command the most social prestige. As we saw in the previous chapter, the thinking of the men who developed the standing moral theories was shaped by their participation in several of these practices.

What would happen, though, if we decided that what women know is just as authoritative as the knowledge of socially prestigious men? A large part of the feminist project has been to legitimate women's knowledge—to insist that what can be learned from women's less prestigious practices ought to be taken just as seriously as what can be learned from the experience of men. In particular, feminist ethicists have explored women's practices to see what kind of *moral* knowledge lurks there.

5.1. The Ethics of Care

And this is how care comes into the picture. In the United States, but also in many other societies, women do far more unpaid, hands-on caregiving than men—they change the diapers, wash the dishes, clean the bathrooms, do the shopping, take the dog to the vet, feed and dress the children, take care of sick or disabled family members, and provide long-term care for elderly relatives. Even when married women have full-time jobs, they still do the vast majority of the housework, child care, and elder care. According to a 2002 study conducted by the Institute for Social Research at the University of Michigan, women spend approximately 27 hours per week on housework while men spend 16 hours per week—a difference of 60 percent. The Family Caregiver Alliance reports that between 60 and 75 percent of unpaid elder and patient care is done by women, and the sociologists Eleanor Maccoby and Robert Mnookin's 1992 study of families in California indicates that after a divorce or in cases where the parents never married, roughly 75 percent of dependent children live with and are cared for by their mothers rather than their fathers—a figure that approaches 100 percent when the children are infants or toddlers. Paid caregivers are mostly women, too. Almost 96 percent of professional nurses are women, and the percentage of women providing day care for children is close to 99 percent. The practice of care, then, is overwhelmingly a woman's practice.

Suppose we take this practice seriously, as if it were just as important as the practice of law or medicine. How does caregiving shape the thinking of those who engage in it? And even more to the point, for present purposes, how does caregiving shape its practitioners' *moral* thinking? That's a big question, because there are so many different forms that caregiving can take and so many different circumstances under which care is given. So let's whittle it down, temporarily, to the practice of mothering. It's not that mothering is paradigmatic of women's work—there are plenty of women, after all, who aren't mothers—but mothering is a form of caregiving that most of us have received and all of us are familiar with, so it's a good place to start. Then we can ask what kind of moral thinking is involved in the caregiving that mothers do. Since every practice has a point, we can begin by thinking about the point of mothering, because that shows us something about the standards we could use to judge whether someone is doing the work of mothering well or badly. Once we've taken a snapshot of that particular practice, we can use what we've learned to make some general observations about other kinds of caregiving. In coming at the question this way, we develop an ethics of care.

The Point of Mothering

Broadly speaking, the point of mothering is to bring about the child's well-being. But this can be broken down into three different kinds of responsibilities. The first (and maybe the most important) is *protection*—the responsibility of keeping the child safe from harm. When you mother a child, you are supposed to see to it that she doesn't run out into the street, eat poisonous substances, fall out the window, become the victim of a child molester, and so on. Protection requires preemptive thinking: You have to be alert to possible sources of danger in the child's environment and try to keep the child from being hurt by them. Sometimes, one of the sources of danger is the mother herself. Sara Ruddick tells the story of Julie, whose ten-month-old baby wouldn't sleep. For the first four months the baby was awake every other hour, day and night, around the clock, and for the six months after that she slept no more than two hours at a time. The father's work frequently kept him from home, so Julie was often alone with the baby. One night she woke—again—to hear the baby screaming, but this time as she approached the crib, her throat constricted and she pictured herself lifting the baby and throwing her at the window, then watching the glass smash and the baby hitting the pavement three stories below. Sickened by these thoughts, Julie wrapped the baby carefully and rode with her on the bus all night from one end of the city to the other, thinking the child would be safe with her if they weren't alone. Julie did what she could to protect her baby, and as Ruddick (1989) remarks, "What she did was enough" (67).

The second responsibility of mothering is *nurturance*. If children need protection, they also need to grow, so mothers must foster that growth. This is partly a matter of providing food, clothing, and shelter, but it also involves giving comfort, love, trust, and respect, so that the child can develop spiritually as well as physically. Nurturance requires concrete thinking: You have to be receptive to *this* particular child's needs. Let's suppose, for example, that your thirteen-year-old son Andy keeps leaving his bike lying at the side of the driveway instead of putting it in the shed where it belongs. You remind him to the point of nagging, but he always "forgets." So you start thinking concretely, imagining, as well as you can, what it's like to be Andy. Lately he's been having bad dreams, and as you reflect on this it strikes you that these dreams have all had a fairly prominent spider motif. You wonder, Are there spiders in the shed? And is he afraid of spiders? You ask him and he says, "Yeah," but you can see, because you're paying careful attention, that he's ashamed to be afraid of such a trivial thing. Now that you know what's wrong, you can figure out how to respond. The kind of nurturance he needs from you is help in overcoming his fear, plus a way to regain his self-respect. So you make a concrete suggestion: You'll give him a broom and go with him to the shed to keep him company while he chases the spiders away. And if he's not quite up for that, you'll chase the spiders yourself while he keeps *you* company.

The third responsibility is *training*, so that the child can live well in the society of others. It includes toilet training; teaching the child to speak; drilling table manners into her; setting limits on her behavior; helping her exercise her capacity for kindness, honesty, and respect; asking her (for the thousandth time) to please shut the door; showing her how to be morally reliable as well as socially savvy. Training requires reflexive thinking: You have to examine your own values to see which ones are faulty and need to be discarded rather than passed on, and you have to examine your motives for disciplining, intervening in, turning a blind eye toward, or insisting on a particular bit of behavior. You must have confidence in your own judgments so that you don't always cave in to social pressure instead of doing what you think you should, but you also have to understand how much power you have over your child so that you don't bully or dominate her. If you always give way, you're *abdicating* your power, which is a way of relinquishing responsibility. That produces the fluttering, ineffectual mother, the emotionally distant mother, the mom who treats her ten-year-old daughter like a girlfriend. If you *abuse* your power, then instead of showing the child how to be a morally responsible person, you'll train her by force, which, in Ruddick's (1989) words, "is more like battle than love" (118). The abuse of power produces the stage mother, the mom who disciplines by yelling and hitting, and the rigid perfectionist. Guarding against both the abdication and the abuse of maternal power requires a kind of hardheaded trust—self-trust as well as trust in the child. The trust is hardheaded because it can't be indiscriminate. It has to be critical; if it isn't, you won't be appropriately angry at yourself when you've been unreliable, or angry at your child when he lets you down.

Our exploration of the point of mothering and the kind of thinking it requires doesn't just show us how to give this kind of care—it shows us how to do it *well*. The reason is that the standards or values for assessing the performance of any practice are right there inside the practice. Some of these are standards for doing the practice correctly in the technical sense. Others, as we'll see in a moment, are *ethical* standards, telling you the morally right or admirable way to do it.

General Features of Care

Now that we've looked at the point of one practice of care, we can use what we saw there to make some general observations about other practices of care: care of poor or homeless people, mental health care, nursing care, care of frail elderly people, home care for people with serious disabilities, hospice care, social work, outpatient care, and so on. What does our snapshot of mothering show us about responsible caregiving in general?

The first thing it shows is that caring well both requires and is an expression of a **caring relationship.** You have to care *about* the person you care *for,* so that the caregiving doesn't become impersonal, cold, or self-serving. Let's say that ever since your mother died, your dad's house has been a mess and he hasn't been eating properly. Because you don't want people to think you're neglecting him, you arrange for a housekeeper, but you draw the line at visiting him and you don't think about him very much except when you write the monthly check for the housekeeper's salary. Are you taking care of him? Yes. Are you taking *good* care of him? No, because you aren't doing it in a caring manner. To care in this sense is to feel concern for your charge (the philosopher Eva Kittay's term for the person receiving the care), which is to say that a caring relationship engages the emotions. As we saw in the story of Julie, though, the relationship shouldn't be sentimentalized into a gooey mess of tender feelings. Some of the emotions it engages are homicidal, and then caring well requires you to stop yourself from acting on your feelings. At other times, caring well requires you to *express* your anger, grief, or frustration, because that's what lets you stay connected to the person in your care. Notice that in the way I'm using the word here, "caring" doesn't just refer to the emotions; as the philosopher Virginia Held points out, it's also a *moral* term. It's a good thing to care about others—a bad thing when we don't. Because it's a moral term, we can use it to guide how and when to act on our feelings, as well as to evaluate specific instances of caregiving.

The second thing our snapshot of mothering shows us is that the caring relationship requires **engagement with another's will**—if you care about the person you are caring for, you interact with him not simply as an object of your care, but as someone with wants, intentions, and desires of his own. You don't high-handedly impose your own will on your charge, riding roughshod over his wishes, because that would be an abuse of the power you have over him. To prevent that abuse, the educator Nel Noddings calls on caregivers to practice *engrossment,* which consists of such close attention to the feelings, needs, ideas, or wants of their charges that the caregivers' own needs and wants are displaced. Good caregivers, she says, "try to apprehend the reality of the other." "My motive energy flows toward the other and perhaps, although not necessarily, toward his ends. . . . I allow my motive energy to be shared; I put it at the service of the other" (Noddings 1984, 33). Engrossment is a way of opening yourself up to your charge, letting yourself be filled with how things are for him, who he is, what he wants. It's setting your own clamoring self to one side so that you can meet *his* needs rather than your own.

The third thing our snapshot of mothering shows is that caring well requires you to **pay attention to the particulars** rather than being guided by abstract thinking. Suppose you work as an aide in the Alzheimer's unit of a nursing home. You believe in the principle of respect for autonomy, and since people can't exercise their autonomy when they're deceived, you think it's wrong to lie to the nursing-home residents. For the same reason, you think it's wrong to humor them in their delusions. One day, however, as you walk down the hall you see an elderly resident having an animated conversation with the image of a lady in hoopskirts and a bonnet that forms a part of the design of the wallpaper. If you were to act on your principle of refusing to collaborate in the residents' dementia, you'd go to her and explain that the lady on the wall isn't real. But in *this* case, with *this* resident, you can see that the delusion is harmless and the resident is having a lovely time, so you walk on by. By thinking about this resident in particular, rather than about morality in general, you provide her with morally admirable care. This isn't to say that you must never engage in abstract thinking. But as Noddings (1984) puts it, "We keep our objective thinking tied to a relational stake at the heart of caring. When we fail to do this, we can climb into clouds of abstraction, moving rapidly away from the caring situation into a domain of objective and impersonal problems where we are free to impose structure as we will. If I do not turn away from my abstractions, I lose the one cared-for. Indeed, I lose myself as one-caring, for I now care about a problem instead of a person" (36).

Thinking Critically about the Ethics of Care

All right so far? Actually, no. Just look at the picture we've created of the morally responsible caregiver. It seems that we have cleverly and painstakingly reinvented the sexist stereotype of the self-effacing housewife who is all wrapped up in her husband and kids and who doesn't bother her pretty little head about public affairs. (This is an instance of Lindemann's ad hoc rule Number 58: Sometimes when you reinvent the wheel you end up with a flat tire.) In fact, a number of feminist ethicists have argued (repeatedly) that each of the three central features of the ethics of care reinforces the womanly stereotype, prescribing courses of action and ways of thinking that ought to be condemned. First, because the caregiver is supposed to care about her charge, she's *open to exploitation*. Second, because the caregiver is supposed to engross herself in the needs and wants of her charge, she's *in danger of losing her integrity*. And third, because the caregiver is supposed to focus on the particular needs and circumstances of her charge, she's *oblivious to the broader concerns of social justice*. These are precisely the harms inflicted on women by the gendered power system that favors men, and for that reason alone the ethics should presumably be resisted rather than embraced. Can the ethics of care be saved? *Should* it be saved? Let's take up each problem in turn and see what can be done about it.

The Problem of Exploitation. Suppose your widowed grandmother suffers from rheumatoid arthritis, and the disease has progressed to the point where she can't scrub floors, do the laundry, or carry heavy grocery bags anymore. Your parents have moved to another city, so that leaves you and your two brothers to give her the care she needs. As it happens, though, neither of your brothers is willing to do his fair share of the necessary shopping and cleaning, and they don't see why you should do it either. They think your grandmother should sell the house in which she's lived for fifty years and move to the city where your parents live so that your mother can take care of her. But you feel a loving concern for your grandmother that won't let you accept this solution. Guided by the ethics of care, you believe that caring about her is a good thing—something you ought to do. So you respond to her needs, taking seriously her desire to remain in familiar surroundings as long as possible. And this puts you in the position of being exploited by your brothers. You have to care about your grandmother even if they don't, which leaves you to shoulder a burden that should, in fairness, be divided equally among all three grandchildren.

Kittay's solution to the problem of exploitation is to call for financial, economic, and logistical support for caregivers (she calls them "dependency workers"). Kittay argues in *Love's Labor* (1999) that if you start from the fact of human dependency instead of from the assumption that "all men are created equal," then giving care to those who must depend on others for support can be seen as one of the requirements of justice. And because dependency workers must themselves depend on other people for support, caring for *them* can also be seen as a requirement of justice. She thinks that we'll know better what form this state-funded support should take after we see more of the consequences of insisting that society has a responsibility to help dependency workers. The philosopher Diemut Bubeck has a different solution. Like Kittay, she points out that women do a vastly disproportionate amount of the work of care and that this is morally unjustifiable, but unlike Kittay, Bubeck thinks the way to stop exploiting caregivers is to require respite care as a duty of citizenship. Her idea, modeled on military service, is that men and women alike would spend some period of their lives in a "caring service" whose mission would be to provide backup care for unpaid dependency workers. Either of these solutions would keep you from being too badly exploited as you take care of your grandmother, and they might even alter your brothers' understanding of their own responsibilities, both to their grandmother and to you.

The Problem of Integrity. Here's a real-life example of how the ethics of care can pose a threat to the caregiver's integrity. Teresa Stangl, the wife of the Kommandant of the concentration camp at Treblinka, was an anti-Nazi and a devout Catholic. She was horrified by what she knew of her husband's job, but even so she maintained a home for him to return to when he could. By providing her husband with domestic comfort, Stangl probably made it easier for him to carry out the Nazis' murderous agenda, yet the ethics of care seemingly requires her to take up this attitude of "not my will but thine be done." Isn't engrossment a matter of displacing your own concerns, needs, and desires with those of the person you care for? If so, what are you supposed to do when a conflict arises between your charge's wants and purposes and your own sense of what's right? Does the ethics of care require you to sacrifice your integrity?

One solution that some feminist ethicists have proposed is to build self-care into the ethics of care so that it doesn't become an ethics of self-erasure. This solution only works, though, if you are caring for yourself for the right reason. If you've dedicated yourself so completely to your Nazi husband that your only motive for taking care of yourself is that it lets you take better care of him, you stand in danger of losing yourself altogether. But if you take care of yourself because you care about *yourself,* you won't lose sight of your own needs—including the need to do what you think is right. Cheshire Calhoun argues that integrity isn't just the personal virtue of holding fast to the moral values that are central to your sense of who you are. She thinks it's also a social virtue, which you exercise by standing for your own best moral judgments *to other people.* Standing up for your best judgments is a way of being reliable. Others can count on you not to fold under pressure, or, since nobody's perfect, they know that if you do fold momentarily, they can count on you to be sorry and do your best to repair the damage. A notion of integrity that consists of this kind of accountability to others isn't compatible with doing what you know is wrong. Care arises from *engaging* with another's will—not sacrificing your own.

The Problem of Obliviousness to Social Justice. Because the ethics of care tells you to pay attention to the particulars of a given interpersonal relationship rather than to be guided by abstract thinking, Claudia Card complains in a 1990 essay in *Hypatia* that it can't help us resist the evil that strangers do to strangers. Not only does the ethics' "up close and personal" focus leave us too nearsighted to see sexism, racism, homophobia, ethnocentrism, and disregard for future generations, says Card, it also offers only patchwork solutions to the problems of world hunger, war, and homelessness. This is a complaint about the *scope* of the ethics of care. It doesn't cover enough of the moral terrain.

The political scientist Joan Tronto's solution to this problem is to redraw the boundary that political theorists and others have marked between morality and politics. Since care is a practice embedded in social life, she claims, it has to be understood in a political context and not just a moral one. Defining care as "a species activity that includes everything that we do to maintain, continue, and repair our 'world' so that we can live in it as well as possible" (Tronto 1993, 103), she rejects the idea that care is restricted to human interaction and that it must take place in a relationship between two individuals. Societies as well as individuals can care about homelessness, for example, and the mechanic who fixes your transmission is giving care to your car. But because Tronto agrees with Card that care isn't a broad enough moral idea to solve the problems of our responsibilities to distant strangers, social inequalities, and the irresponsibility that goes hand-in-hand with privilege, she thinks that the ethics of care is incomplete without the *politics* of care. Such a politics recognizes and supports the caring labor that's crucial to the existence of society. It shifts the goals of social policy from preserving autonomy to fostering interdependence; from promoting interests to meeting needs. It values citizens even when they aren't self-sufficient. And as a practice, care produces not only morally praiseworthy people, but better citizens in a democracy as well.

You'll have to decide for yourself how well these solutions work and whether some of them might distort the ethics in ways that are undesirable. Held and Ruddick, for example, think that Tronto's definition of care is too broad, claiming that once you go beyond person-to-person relationships you're doing something other than the ethics of care. Some feminists think that even if these solutions are the right ones, the ethics is still objectionable because it's basically an ethics for white, middle-class women—the ones who are preoccupied with kids and carpools and a nice house in the suburbs. That's not how the sociologist Patricia Hill Collins sees it, though. She argues that the care ethic is visible in the African American practice of "othermothering"—looking after the children in the community through networks of grandmothers, cousins, aunts, and neighbors who share this responsibility with the biological mother. Collins also sees the ethics in the call-and-response pattern of speech used in traditional African American church services: The preacher makes a claim that's appraised and affirmed by the congregation, in a back-and-forth, emotional expression of selves-in-relation.

5.2. Feminist Responsibility Ethics

While the ethics of care is probably the best-known body of feminist theory, it's not the only one. Care ethics is based on a morally crucial relationship between people that has too often been ignored or dismissed by nonfeminist ethicists, but relationships other than those involving care are also morally important, and they too give rise to responsibilities. Nor are relationships the only source of the moral demands made on us. For these reasons, several feminist ethicists have gone beyond care to develop a broader ethics of responsibility.

Margaret Urban Walker isn't so much interested in the abstract questions that philosophers have traditionally raised about the conditions under which someone is morally responsible (Was he free to act otherwise? Did she form the proper intention?) as she is in examining how responsibility works in practice. If you look carefully at how people "do" responsibility, you'll see something amazingly intricate. For starters, there's the rich variety of actions that fall within this category. You're willing to be the designated driver—a way of *taking* responsibility. You acknowledge paternity—a way of *accepting* responsibility. You blame your parents for your lousy life—a way of *deflecting* responsibility. You give your brother-in-law an alibi—a way of *redirecting* responsibility. You say, "None of this would have happened if you'd kept your big mouth shut"—a way of *assigning* responsibility. You ask your co-worker to cover for you—a way of *renegotiating* responsibility. And that's just the beginning. We hold people to their promises, excuse them, demand an explanation, give them a standing ovation, let them stew in their own juice, award them the Nobel Prize, and sentence them to death by lethal injection.

These activities are accompanied by a rich array of *feelings:* regret, indignation, delight, shame, pride, satisfaction, grief, hope, anxiety, or fear. There are conventional *ways* of apologizing or excusing yourself, raising someone's expectations, offering compensation, and taking the credit. And there are a number of different things *for which* we hold ourselves and each other responsible: tasks, roles, acts, the failure to act, outcomes of action beyond our control, habits, attitudes, and other people.

Notice how dynamic all of this is. It's like a very complicated snowball fight involving many players. Some throw, some duck, some are hit, some build fortifications, some team up, some keep making new snowballs, and the little kids run around getting in the way. Actually, though, it's even more complex than this analogy allows, because *how* you are supposed to participate in your society's practices of responsibility depends just as much on your gender, class, age, ethnicity, and race as it does on your own achievements. The matter of who gets to do what to whom is largely determined by the social power that's distributed according to these demographics, and so is the matter of who has to account to whom. To return to a consideration that came up in the discussion of identities, if you're the president of the company you can lay off half the workforce; if you're the cleaning woman, you can't. By the same token, a Latino laborer is much more likely to be drug-tested than is a white stockbroker. And just as social position influences whether and to what extent you may take responsibility, assign responsibility, or avoid responsibility, so too it plays a role in determining who gets to set or change the rules that govern the practice. An ethics of responsibility, then, can accommodate *group* as well as individual responsibilities.

As Walker points out, though, practices of responsibility are often rigged. The social forces that allow some people to take responsibility for the things that are fun or rewarding, while imposing on other people the kinds of responsibility that keep them from enjoying many of the good things in life, are the same forces that hide the fact that this is going on.

Some of these forces *naturalize* the uneven distribution of responsibility. Mothering is a great example of this: It's women's nature to care for children because they have a biologically hardwired maternal instinct while men, of course, don't. By making this arrangement seem to be a function of biological determinism, its coercive nature is kept largely hidden from view. By the same token, women are "naturally" better at cleaning up after the party, soothing hurt feelings, and getting hot meals on the table. (Okay, there's one legitimate exception here: Women really *are* naturally better at shopping for shoes.)

Other forces *privatize* unfair assignments of responsibility. Gays and lesbians, for example, are supposed to keep their sex lives private, since it's "not appropriate" for them to hold hands in public or do the other things straight people do that show they're with somebody. The "don't ask, don't tell" policy for gays in the military hides the fact that gays are in constant danger of being drummed out of the service, by making it appear reasonable and good that they should keep their sexual orientation to themselves. Similarly, black people are supposed to stay in their own part of town, since it's not "appropriate" for them to be too visible in white neighborhoods.

Still other forces *normalize* the unfairness. They focus so much attention on the norms or standards for fulfilling a particular responsibility that the question of why *that* kind of person is forced to assume the responsibility is completely hidden from view. Think of the many ways in which girls are taught the norms for looking attractive: Be thin, use gel and a blow-dryer to style your hair, shave your legs, know how to apply makeup and nail polish, be careful how you sit, never smell sweaty, and on and on and on. Incessantly barraging women with the how-tos is a wonderful way of concealing the unfairness of requiring them to take far more responsibility for their appearance than men take for theirs.

Notice that practices of responsibility look forward as well as backward. Card points out that people who have suffered from unfair distributions of responsibility can do more than make backward-looking assignments of blame for past wrongs. A woman who has been raped, for example, can adopt a forward-looking stance that allows her to *take* responsibility for what happened to her—not in the sense of blaming herself, but in the sense of refusing to be a victim. She can be responsible for rebuilding her life at the same time as she holds her attacker responsible for his deed.

But what about the harder cases, where the person who wrongs you doesn't realize that what he's doing is wrong? Normally, of course, adults are expected to know the moral rules and to be aware of the standards by which other people judge them. That's part of what it means to be a morally competent person. But Calhoun observes that morally competent people can be morally *in*competent in abnormal contexts. She's thinking, for instance, of the really thoughtful guy who offers to help his wife with the housework. In the normal moral context, the injustice of assigning the responsibility for vacuuming and dusting on the basis of gender rather than according to who lives there is concealed. (She just naturally cares more about keeping the place clean than he does. Women are better at that sort of thing than men.) Since the normal context is the one this guy operates out of, he can't see the sexism behind his assumption that he's doing something *nice* rather than doing *his share*. That being the case, it hardly seems fair for us to blame him. But feminists inhabit what Calhoun calls an *abnormal* moral context—"abnormal" in the sense that you can see things from it that aren't visible in the normal context, like the sexism in the husband's offer. Because he's morally incompetent in the feminist context, we could excuse him on the same grounds that we excuse young children's wrongdoing—he's not responsible for his attitude because he's still learning the moral rules. But Calhoun thinks we should hold him responsible anyway. When we reproach people who engage in sexist behavior, we teach them that what they're doing is wrong, motivate them to change the way they act, and show that we respect them instead of treating them like children. This is one way in which feminists can *take* responsibility (in Card's sense) for sexism.

A careful look at all the complicated activities that make up our practices of responsibility, says Walker, suggests that morality isn't what the moral theorists working out of the Enlightenment tradition seem to think it is. That tradition offers us a picture of the moral agent as a solitary judge who uses lawlike principles that have been logically deduced from some comprehensive moral theory to figure out what's right and wrong and to make rational choices. It assumes that morality is essentially *knowledge* and that the core of moral knowledge is essentially *theoretical*. It's a picture of general formulas applied to particular cases whose "superfluous" details have been cleared away so that the cases can be sorted into broad types, which makes for uniform judgments. It's a picture of morality as an individually action-guiding system within or for a person.

A feminist ethics of responsibility, by contrast, pictures morality as something we do *together*. It permeates all of social life, so it can't be partitioned off from politics (as Tronto does) or from any other aspect of society. Morality gives us a common vocabulary and a set of shared understandings that we can use to define or contest our responsibilities. As such, says

Walker (1998), it "both presupposes and seeks a continuing common life" (63)—a way of going on together as "us." She calls this an "expressive-collaborative" view of morality. It's expressive in that the intricate dance of taking, deflecting, and assigning responsibility by appealing to socially recognized values is the medium through which we express who we are. It's collaborative in that the goal of morality is not only to *discover* but also to *construct* shared understandings of how to live well together. The test of the moral soundness of these understandings is in the goodness of the social arrangements they produce and the ability of the people within those arrangements to make moral sense of themselves in the life they live together.

These two samples of feminist moral theory display some common themes. Both reject the idea that persons are "punctual" and unconnected, and insist that selves are always nested in webs of relationship. Both emphasize differences among people rather than making abstract generalizations about human nature. Both regard gender as an unjust power system. Both use the language of responsibilities rather than rights or duties. And both begin from careful examinations of actual, real-time personal interactions. This on-the-ground quality is highly characteristic of feminist ethics; it's a way of avoiding the mistake of theorizing from too limited a set of examples. In the next three chapters, however, we're going to get even closer to the ground, to see how feminist ethicists map the gendered terrain of personal and social issues surrounding advances in biomedicine, violence, and globalization.

For Further Reading

Card, Claudia. 1990. "Caring and Evil." Review essay. *Hypatia* 5, no. 1: 101–108.

———. 1996. *The Unnatural Lottery: Character and Moral Luck*. Philadelphia: Temple University Press.

Gilligan, Carol. 1982. *In a Different Voice: Psychological Theory and Women's Development*. Cambridge, MA: Harvard University Press.

Held, Virginia. 1993. *Feminist Morality: Transforming Culture, Society and Politics*. Chicago: University of Chicago Press.

Kittay, Eva Feder. 1999. *Love's Labor: Essays on Women, Equality, and Dependency.* New York: Routledge.

Maccoby, Eleanor E., and Robert H. Mnookin. 1992. *Dividing the Child: Social and Legal Dilemmas of Custody.* Cambridge: Harvard University Press.

Noddings, Nel. 1984. *Caring: A Feminine Approach to Ethics and Moral Education.* Berkeley and Los Angeles: University of California Press.

Ruddick, Sara. 1989. *Maternal Thinking: Toward a Politics of Peace.* Boston: Beacon.

Tronto, Joan. 1993. *Moral Boundaries: A Political Argument for an Ethic of Care.* New York: Routledge.

Walker, Margaret Urban. 1998. *Moral Understandings: A Feminist Study in Ethics.* New York: Routledge.

Part Two

CLOSE-UPS

CHAPTER 6

Feminist Bioethics

If any subfield of ethics has ever been taken up by the general public, bioethics is that field. Scarcely a day goes by without some bioethics story in the news. National commissions are formed regularly to advise the president of the United States on bioethical issues ranging from end-of-life care to stem cell research. Bioethicists make frequent appearances on TV and radio talk shows. Movies and TV dramas frequently incorporate bioethical themes. It's no exaggeration to say that bioethics has become the public face of ethics—the ethical discourse that matters to people in all walks of life, whether they know anything about formal moral theories or not. Bioethics matters to feminists too. But because they bring to it their own moral theories, as well as their pictures of persons, social group relations, and rationality, the result is a bit more interesting and arguably more useful than is bioethics done in a nonfeminist manner.

Unlike medical ethics, which goes back several thousand years and is aimed at guiding physicians' professional conduct, bioethics began in the late 1960s as the United States in particular tried to grapple with ethical and social issues arising from rapid advances in medical technology. There was, for example, the invention of the ventilator, which keeps a body breathing even when natural organ functioning has shut down and brain activity has stopped. According to the traditional heart–lung criteria for determining death, the person on the ventilator is alive, because the heart is pumping and the lungs are oxygenating the person's blood. And the person certainly looks alive—she's warm to the touch, her chest rises and falls, and unless her skin is very dark it has a pinkish rather than a grayish hue. How long, though, should these signs of life be maintained?

And if doctors disconnect her from the ventilator, are they killing her? Would it be morally permissible to remove her kidneys and other organs if they could benefit someone else, or would that be killing her too? Is there anything ethically fishy about switching, in the face of questions like these, to a brain-death criterion for determining death?

The consumer rights movement of the 1960s, like the patient rights movement that grew out of it, emphasized consumers' right to determine for themselves what kinds of medical treatments they were willing to be subjected to. Bioethicists put this right into Kantian language, urging physicians to respect their patients' autonomy and claiming that patients had the right to refuse treatment even if that refusal meant certain death. Physicians who force on patients their own ideas of what is in the patients' best interest, bioethicists argued, act paternalistically, making personal and value-laden decisions for patients that only patients themselves are entitled to make.

The Tuskegee syphilis study, conducted for forty years by the U.S. Public Health Service, involved 400 men with syphilis and 200 uninfected men who served as controls. Begun in 1932 in Macon County, Alabama, it was a "study in nature" intended to track the course of untreated syphilis in black men, to see if race was a factor in how the disease behaved. The research subjects, many of them uneducated sharecroppers, were told that they had "bad blood" and that the painful spinal taps they endured (so that researchers could monitor the progression of the disease) would cure them. Even more shamefully, when penicillin became widely available after the Second World War as the standard treatment for the disease, steps were taken to prevent these men from receiving it. The scandal broke in 1972, when the *New York Times* and other media made public what the researchers had been doing. Bioethicists again put the ethical issue in Kantian language, arguing that the research subjects' autonomy had been violated and that experiments on human subjects must not go forward without the subjects' freely given, informed consent.

In 1973 the Supreme Court handed down its landmark decision *Roe v. Wade*. In it, Justice Harry Blackmun declared that the constitutionally protected right to privacy includes a woman's right to terminate a pregnancy up to the time when her fetus is "viable"—that is, capable of surviving outside the uterus. Bioethicists were not quite so divided over this decision as was the rest of the nation. Daniel Callahan, for example, thought that because fetuses aren't persons (though they are morally valuable), a woman could in good conscience choose an abortion. Mary Ann Warren listed five traits—the ability to feel pain, the ability to reason, intentional activity, the capacity for communication, and self-awareness—that she took to be central to personhood, and argued from these that as fetuses aren't persons, abortion is permissible. Judith Jarvis Thomson claimed that even if fetuses *were* full-fledged persons, neither they nor anyone else has the right to use another person's body to sustain their lives, so women were free to abort them. Don Marquis, however, argued that it's just as wrong to kill a fetus as it is to kill an adult human being, because what is wrong-making about either kind of killing is that the victim is deprived of "a future like ours."

And then came the advances in reproductive medicine. In 1978 Louise Brown, the first "test-tube baby," was born in England after having been conceived by in-vitro fertilization (IVF). Because her mother's blocked fallopian tubes kept her father's sperm from reaching her eggs, doctors made a small incision in her mother's lower abdomen, extracted several eggs, and united them with sperm in a petrie dish. Once the fertilized eggs began dividing, one of the resulting embryos was implanted in Mrs. Brown's uterus and nature was allowed to take its course. The public reaction to Louise's birth was not unlike what the reaction would be now if a human clone were born: fascinated repulsion, pronouncements that the doctors were "playing God," and worries that this would be the end of family life as we know it, while entrepreneurs quietly cashed in on the technology as they set up IVF clinics around the world. At around the same time, amniocentesis and fetal monitoring began to be used routinely, and sperm banks were established to facilitate artificial insemination by anonymous "donors" (vendors, really, as they are paid for their sperm), all of which raised questions about who had what sorts of responsibilities to the children born with the aid of these technologies.

Advances in genetic knowledge have not yet been translated into useful therapies, but that hasn't stopped bioethicists from worrying about them. Is it ethical for researchers to patent animals whose genes they have altered? Who is entitled to genetic information about you—your sister? your boss? your insurance company? Now that there is a genetic test for Huntington's chorea, a debilitating and dementing late-onset disease, if it runs in your family, do you owe it to yourself to find out if you have the gene for it? Are your children entitled to know?

Employment has been the primary source of health care insurance since the Second World War, when companies operating under federal wage and price controls added health care benefits as a means of attracting workers. That fact, plus the steadily climbing cost of health care, raises serious ethical issues about access to care. As employers grow more reluctant to absorb the increased costs and health care is increasingly privatized by for-profit corporations, fewer people will be able to afford the care they want or need. Yet in 2004, health care spending in the United States reached $1.8 trillion. That's 15.5 percent of the gross domestic product—more than the United States spends on defense and education combined. At the same time, some 44 million people, roughly 15 percent of the population, have no health care insurance at all, while another 60 million or so are badly underinsured. What, if anything, does a society owe those who can't afford to pay for health care? What's the fairest way of distributing health care benefits, and which benefits should be distributed when money must also be spent on other goods and services?

6.1. Bioethics in the Dominant Mode

Most nonfeminist bioethicists have tackled questions like these pretty much the way the rest of us do—by swapping moral intuitions that they believe are widely shared. However, when they appeal to theory to back up those intuitions, they tend to rely on the moral and political theories that dominate ethics in general. So, for example, Norman Daniels bases his arguments for equal access to health care on John Rawls's *Theory of Justice,* which itself draws heavily on Kant. In his classic article, "Active and Passive Euthanasia,"

James Rachels argues as a utilitarian: The benefits of directly killing terminally ill patients in many cases outweigh the burdens of letting them die. In another classic, *Deciding for Others,* Allen Buchanan and Dan Brock invoke two well-known ethical principles, one Kantian and the other utilitarian, when they argue that doctors must strike a balance between *respect for patient autonomy* and *fostering patient well-being* as they try to determine if a patient is competent to make treatment decisions for herself.

These two principles—respect for autonomy and beneficence, or well-being—have an honorable history within bioethics. They are among four important bioethical principles identified by Tom Beauchamp and James Childress in their widely known *Principles of Biomedical Ethics,* now in its fifth edition. When they wrote that book in the late 1970s, Beauchamp and Childress were worried about a potentially serious problem: Was the correct moral theory for guiding the practice of medicine one that focused, like Kantian ethics, on rights and duties, or one that weighed the consequences of an action, like utilitarianism? And if there could be no agreement about that, was a biomedical ethics even possible? Their way of solving the problem was to argue that it doesn't matter if we disagree about whether rights-based or consequentialist moral theories are the ones that ought to show us what to do, because we can agree on a set of "middle-level" principles—respect for autonomy, beneficence, nonmaleficence (doing no harm), and justice—that can be derived from either kind of moral theory. And they proceeded to demonstrate all the kinds of bioethical work that these four principles can do.

Not all nonfeminist bioethicists endorse middle-level principles, of course. Almost as soon as "principlism" became an established bioethical methodology, it came under attack from people who favored narrative approaches, virtue-based ethics, and other ways of proceeding. I think it's fair to say, however, that the bioethics that commands the greatest respect from hospital administrators, physicians, and government policy makers is centered in one way or another on rights-based or consequence-oriented moral theories.

This well-established mode of bioethics can be characterized by (1) abstract rules and principles, (2) liberal individualism, (3) an elite and socially powerful clientele, and (4) inattention to most forms of oppression. Let's look at each of these features in turn.

1. Abstract Rules and Principles

These rules, derived from the dominant liberal moral theories, pervade bioethics. To see a close-up example, consider this case study, titled "Mother and Son," which appeared recently in the premier journal in the field, the *Hastings Center Report:*

> JJ is a seven-year-old boy who lives with his biological mother in California. JJ has been hyperactive and aggressive for most of his life. He says he has bad thoughts and that he hears voices telling him to kill his mother. He has been diagnosed with post-traumatic stress disorder, bipolar disorder, and impulse control disorder. . . .
>
> In May of 2001, when it appeared that JJ was about to enter yet another round of medication, his mother discovered in the course of her research that medical marijuana might help her son. She knew nothing about the medical use of marijuana and did not support the current movement in California. However, she discussed the option with caseworkers, team members, and several physicians. After consulting with them, she decided to give the treatment a try. She notified JJ's medical team that he was no longer on any psychotropic medications and had begun treatment with medical marijuana, as outlined under California's Proposition 215, or the Compassionate Use Act of 1996. Currently, JJ takes the marijuana in a muffin—one-half of a muffin (containing one-forty-eighth of a cup of pulverized dry leaves) in the morning, and one-half in the afternoon. JJ is monitored by a pediatrician, who adjusts the dosage.
>
> The results have been very good. JJ's social worker and teachers report that his behavior has taken a dramatic turn. His demeanor is very polite and he interacts enthusiastically with staff and students. . . . But the question remains: do parents have the right to allow their children to use medical marijuana, and do physicians have the prerogative to prescribe it in such situations? (Case Study 2002, 11)

The first commentator, Kevin O'Brien, explicitly appeals to the middle-level principles in reaching his conclusions. He points out that both morality and the law respect the *autonomy* of parents to determine medical care for children, arguing that because (1) the marijuana "works with dramatic results," (2) the mother's decision was well researched, and (3) a physician is supervising JJ's care, the mother is behaving in a morally responsible manner. Then he turns to the role of the physician, reminding us that "physicians must above all *do no harm,* and according to the principle of *beneficence,* they must care for the well-being of their patients" (my italics). He talks about the physician's "right and duty" to inform the mother about medical marijuana and explain the drug's foreseeable risks and benefits, and concludes that both mother and doctor are serving JJ's best interests.

The other commentator, Peter A. Clark, takes a more strictly consequentialist approach to the case. He describes it as "a situation that has two consequences—one good and the other evil. In this case, marijuana is more effective than conventional therapies. The evil effect is that marijuana has possible long-term negative effects and might lead to more serious drug abuse." Since the likelihood of JJ's becoming a pothead is reasonably remote and JJ's medication is being carefully monitored, Clark argues that "the benefits outweigh the burdens" and, like O'Brien, concludes that both mother and physician are doing the right thing.

While many feminist bioethicists might agree that the moral actors in this case are behaving well, they would likely be wary of the utilitarian and Kantian theories behind the reasoning that led O'Brien and Clark to this conclusion. Rather than focusing on the mother's rights and physician's prerogatives, a feminist analysis might first track the *responsibilities* that are at issue here, and then assess whether anything is amiss with how those responsibilities are kept in play. Who is responsible for what, and to whom? Who has to account to whom, and why? What kinds of negotiations might be needed to safeguard this child and improve his mental health?

To answer questions like these, a feminist ethics of responsibility bids the people who are responsible for JJ to *collaborate* in his care, rather than standing on their rights. One way to do this is for JJ's mother, pediatrician, and social worker to think about what they should do for JJ in terms of three kinds of stories—stories of identity, stories of relationship, and stories of value. Stories of *identity* allow each deliberator to understand what he or she cares about, responds to, and pays attention to: Knowing what matters to me, where I stand, and what I stand for, is a crucial first step in negotiating with others. Stories of *relationship* allow the deliberators to acknowledge their shared history, to see how that brings them to this point in JJ's care, and to consider what kinds of expectations are set up by the relationships among them. Stories of *value* are histories of the deliberators' shared understandings regarding the moral values that are important here, and *how* important each of them is.

One piece of the story that is missing from the case study is JJ's story. What happened to him in his young life that he should be the victim of post-traumatic stress disorder? Other pieces are missing as well: Is JJ's mother at a disadvantage here because she is a woman and women are "naturally" responsible for whatever happens to their children, including trauma? Where is JJ's father, and what are his responsibilities regarding JJ's care? Why is the bioethicist who wrote this case so worried about giving the boy marijuana? Is JJ poor and black, and might the bioethicist have unacknowledged racist views of black drug users that give rise to his concern? (This is an instance of Lindemann's ad hoc rule Number 17: When somebody—even a bioethicist—hands you a story, pick it up and look at what's underneath.)

After enough of these stories have been told for JJ's caregivers to get a good sense of who they and the other deliberators are, what is going on morally, who is taking care of what, and whether responsibilities have been distributed fairly, they will probably conclude, as the case commentators did, that all is well in JJ's neck of the woods. The difference between what they and nonfeminist deliberators would do, though, is a matter of what they are looking at. By focusing on identities and the moral understandings arising from them, they affirm the moral self-expression and mutual recognition that lie at the heart of the idea that bioethics is something we do *together*.

2. *Liberal Individualism*

With a few notable exceptions such as Daniel Callahan and Ezekiel Emanuel, nonfeminist bioethicists tend to assume that people are essentially self-reliant, self-interested, unconnected to others, and in a position to advocate for what they want. (Sound familiar? This is the picture of the person you met in Chapter Four.) They also assume that, morally speaking, people are interchangeable: What holds for you holds for everybody else in your situation. And they assume that moral judgments are supposed to be impartial, dispassionate, and detached. As a result, their closely reasoned arguments for, say, harvesting the organs of a patient who is irreversibly dying but not yet dead pretty typically involve a generic patient, a faceless staff, no mention of the patient's family, and no hint that the bioethicist is in any way a part of the scenario.

Obviously, a very sick and helpless patient looks nothing like this independent, unconnected, self-interested individual, but bioethicists have expended a great deal of effort on molding patients to fit the liberal ideal. One of the most visible ways they have done it is by promoting the use of *advance directives*—written instructions designating either (a) the kind of medical treatment or (b) the decision maker the person would want if she became so ill that she could no longer decide these matters for herself. The point of an advance directive is that it allows the patient to exercise her autonomy *even when she doesn't have any*, either by appointing a proxy decision maker or by making her own choices ahead of time, while she still can. The presumption that nonfeminist bioethicists have tended to make is that all of us want to approximate the ideal of the autonomous liberal individual, though despite their best efforts, 80 percent of us never draw up an advance directive.

Feminist bioethicists, by contrast, tend to situate patients within the webs of relationships that usually surround them, thereby making visible the family members or other intimates who are most closely involved in their care. Sensitivity to the moral understandings that govern familial relationships, coupled with sensitivity to how gender operates both at the bedside and within families, produces a more nuanced account of how best to respond morally to patients at the end of life.

3. An Elite and Socially Powerful Clientele

Bioethicists serve on presidential commissions; testify before state legislatures; deliver ethics Grand Rounds in teaching hospitals; sit on the ethics committees of medical professional societies, hospitals, pharmaceutical companies, biotech companies, and even NASA; and monitor human subjects research as members of Institutional Review Boards. Whom, then, do they serve? Government officials, hospital administrators, policy makers, physicians, astronauts, scientists, technicians, and big business. While many of them do extremely useful work for that clientele, they are moving in circles of privilege and power—circles that have a definite effect on one's outlook. When you are rubbing shoulders with those who call the shots, you are apt to absorb the shot-callers' values and points of view, and that can make it difficult to retain your own sense of what matters. In fact, your job as a bioethicist can depend on your taking your client's point of view. As the bioethicist Carl Elliott points out,

> It is a rare hospital that will keep on its payroll a clinical ethicist who constantly and publicly criticizes hospital policy. Yet by the same token, it is a rare corporation that will continue to fund bioethicists who are constantly and publicly criticizing corporate policy. This does not mean that corporations are morally suspect. It means that it is not good business to give money to the very people who are criticizing your marketing practices in the developing world, who are calling for a halt to your stem cell research, who are lobbying to place limits on the life of your drug patents, or who are attempting to block your clinical trials. The fact that this is not good business is exactly why bioethicists should be wary. (Elliott 2001, 10–11)

One of the most heavily used tools in the feminist bioethicist's toolkit is attention to social group relations. This gives feminist bioethicists an edge over their nonfeminist colleagues: They are better equipped to mark the moral dangers arising from too prolonged an exposure to the corrosive effect of power.

4. Inattention to Most Forms of Oppression

Nonfeminist bioethics does pay attention to differences among social groups. It laments the lack of access to health care for the working poor—the people who aren't poor enough to qualify for Medicaid but are too poor to afford health insurance. It worries about children's participation in clinical trials, about accommodating the beliefs of religious groups such as Jehovah's Witnesses and Orthodox Jews, about providing long-term care for the elderly. It notes that the Tuskegee experiments targeted African Americans and that people who are mentally ill often fail to receive adequate care.

What this bioethics doesn't do, though, is take account of how different social groups *oppress* one another. It has had little to say about the social forces that require some social groups to serve the interests of other, more powerful groups, or that push groups out of mainstream society altogether. It tends to ignore the power dynamics of race, class, gender, sexual orientation, and ethnicity. The major exception to this lack of attention has been in the area of disability. In *From Chance to Choice: Genetics and Justice,* for example, Allen Buchanan, Dan Brock, Norman Daniels, and Dan Wikler—very influential bioethicists indeed—devote a chapter to the objections against genetic medicine that have been voiced by disability rights activists. Disability is, of course, one of the conditions that medicine is supposed to prevent or alleviate, and that may explain why bioethicists care about how disabled people are treated even when they don't pay much attention to bad treatment caused by social attitudes toward other kinds of difference. It's not simply that nonfeminist bioethicists have by and large failed to ask about the impact of racism, sexism, and ethnocentrism on health care—and this is despite well-known data about the relevance of race, gender, and class to things like pain management and cardiac care—but that they haven't availed themselves of the methodologies developed by critical race theorists, queer theorists, and feminists. And that's where, in particular, a feminist bioethics comes in.

6.2. Bioethics in a Feminist Mode

What does a feminist bioethics look like? It's a bioethics that examines how power in the guise of gender, race, and other forms of oppression plays itself out in health care practice and the theory that surrounds that practice. It undertakes this examination not only by asking, Where are the women in this picture? but also by using feminist theories of knowledge, rationality, selfhood, society, and so on as it grapples with the ethical issues surrounding health care. Let me demonstrate with a feminist analysis of four such issues: (1) the doctor–patient relationship, (2) physician-assisted suicide, (3) abortion, and (4) allocation of health care resources. If you're wondering why you can't find reproductive technologies in this list, the answer is that feminist bioethics is too often seen as "about" women's plumbing. I want to show you that it's about a great deal more than that.

The Doctor–Patient Relationship

Much of the bioethics literature on the ethics that should guide the doctor–patient relationship is case-driven, so let's take a look at another case:

> Al Brown is a seventy-three-year-old man with cerebral palsy and severe spastic paralysis in all four limbs. He was admitted to a dependent care facility forty years ago and has lived there ever since. Despite his significant physical impairment and need for assistance with basic life functions, he is cognitively intact.
>
> Several years ago, Mr. Brown was given phenobarbital for treatment of a seizure disorder. When the threat of seizures subsided, he continued to receive 60 milligrams of phenobarbitol four times a day. Now, each time a new pharmacist or physician is assigned to his unit, phenobarbitol levels are drawn. These invariably run in the 50s in micrograms per milliliter, suggesting to clinicians that his dosage should be reduced. Mr. Brown objects to the reduction, stating that he is

doing fine, has not had any seizures, and "always gets messed up when people fool around with my medications." (Mahowald 1996, 107)

Mary Mahowald has analyzed this case using feminist standpoint theory—the theory that the standpoint of an oppressed people is superior to the standpoint of the oppressor, in that it takes seriously what the dominant standpoint glosses over or dismisses. In the case of Mr. Brown, we can see the knowledge of the health care professionals as dominant, while what Mr. Brown knows about the amount of phenobarbital that works best for him is apt not to get registered by the health care professionals as knowledge at all. The professionals, who know authoritatively what the proper dosage is, will likely discount Mr. Brown as an ignorant layman who lacks scientific training and is unfamiliar with the risks reported in the medical literature. Moreover, if Mr. Brown continues to insist on the 60-milligram dose, his physician might begin to pathologize him, explaining away the insistence by supposing that Mr. Brown has a psychological need to draw attention to himself or to exert undue amounts of control over his health care providers.

As a number of feminist epistemologists have argued, the ability to know things authoritatively is dependent on social position: It requires a certain standing within the knower's community. What a scientist can know, for example, and with whom she can work to advance knowledge, depends crucially on how she is situated vis-à-vis other authoritative knowers. Nor is social situation relevant only to science. A sense of competence regarding what we know about ourselves and our relationships to others, about the world and our personal possibilities for living well in it, also requires social standing within the community of those who know. Those who don't possess that standing—as is typically true of women or, in this case, patients—have often been ignored, belittled, or dismissed.

Because Mr. Brown doesn't have the requisite social standing, he lacks the ability to know authoritatively. He probably never acquired a college education, let alone a medical or pharmaceutical degree, and from the way he speaks we can guess that he is probably not a member of a privileged social class. Moreover, he is a patient, and disabled. But if his physicians dismiss what he knows from his own experience about his body's reaction to phenobarbital solely because he occupies a lower position than they do in the cognitive hierarchy, they are doing something morally wrong.

Thinking you know more than someone else isn't in itself a moral failing; a physician generally *does* have expertise the patient lacks, and where medicine is concerned, patients would generally prefer to trust a physician's knowledge over their own. To the extent, however, that a physician discounts a patient's experience because the patient is the physician's *social* inferior, the validity of the physician's claim to authority is weakened. The doctor–patient relationship that was previously just a hierarchy starts to become an oppressive hierarchy, no different morally from the sexist hierarchy that permits powerful men to discredit a woman's judgment just because she is a woman.

By contrast, the physician who begins from the standpoint of the patient, respecting the patient's judgments about his bodily experience, the character of his daily life, what conduces to his happiness, and the other considerations that can be brought to bear on his condition, is then able to enter into a collaboration with this patient. Working together, they can construct an understanding of what the patient is doing and thinking, and what constitutes an optimal medical response.

Physician-Assisted Suicide

Feminist bioethicists have argued that the dominant way of thinking about the ethics of physician-assisted suicide—as a conflict between the doctor's duty of nonmaleficence and the patient's right to autonomy—is too individualistic, in that it misses the way gender and other social forces affect patients' requests to die. The lawyer-bioethicist Susan M. Wolf, for example, worries that because women have been socialized to selfless devotion and care for others, they may seek physician-assisted dying as a way to avoid burdening their family with their own care. Concerned that too little attention is being paid to the failures of relationships and resources that make suicide seem like a woman's best remaining option, and concerned too that "problems we know to be correlated with gender—difficulty getting good medical care generally, poor pain relief, a higher incidence of depression, and a higher rate of poverty—may figure more prominently in women's motivation" than men's, she concludes that the cultural context is too oppressive to justify the legalization of physician-assisted suicide at this time (Wolf 1996, 283).

Another feminist bioethicist, Jennifer Parks, argues from the same premises to the opposite conclusion. Like Wolf, Parks believes that we have to look beyond the patient's right to autonomy and the doctor's duty of nonmaleficence by paying attention to the gendered context in which patients' requests for doctor-assisted suicide take place. And Parks agrees with Wolf that "valorization of women's self-sacrifice" and "background sexism" pose a danger here. But whereas Wolf thinks the danger is that women's requests for assisted suicide will be too enthusiastically granted, Parks thinks the danger is that their requests will be trivialized, dismissed, or ignored.

Parks is worried about the same thing that worries Mary Mahowald in the case of Mr. Brown: Oppression strips people of the ability to know authoritatively. A woman may know that her life is "burdensome, meaningless, and no longer worth living," says Parks (2000) but what she knows is easily discounted as irrational in a social world where women are seen as emotional rather than thinking beings (31). She points to a review by the bioethicists Steven Miles and Alison August (1990) of "right to die" court cases, in which patients or their proxies asked for life-sustaining treatment to be withdrawn. When the patient was a man, the courts honored the requests in 75 percent of the reported cases, as opposed to only 14 percent of cases where the patient was a woman. Miles and August underscored the language of the courts: Men's requests tended to be characterized as "rational," "carefully considered," "appropriate to the circumstances," whereas women's were labeled "irrational," "impulsive," and "transient." Given how gender un-authorizes what women know, especially if they are further disadvantaged by race, age, or poverty, Parks argues that their requests for aid in dying must be taken seriously. An additional way in which Parks might have turned Wolf's point on its head, but didn't, would have been to ask how many women who have been socialized to care for others would *like* to end it all but are kept from it by their selfless devotion to their families.

Abortion

If you were a Martian unfamiliar with human life forms and you happened to be reading a typical nonfeminist bioethicist's arguments regarding abortion, you would have no idea that fetuses grow inside women's bodies. As the feminist sociologist Barbara Katz Rothman pointed out as long ago as 1986, amniocentesis, ultrasound, and other fetal monitoring technologies have increasingly allowed us to visualize the fetus as an isolated individual floating in space, rather than as a developing organism intimately connected to and part of a woman's body. The political scientist Rosalind Pollack Petchesky (1987) claims that anti-abortion activists often use images of a late-stage fetus inside the womb to attempt to force public recognition of "the foetus as primary and autonomous, the women as absent or peripheral" (271), but even bioethicists who think abortion should be permitted have treated fetuses as if they grew under a cabbage leaf. Callahan crops the pregnant woman out of the picture by looking solely at the moral worth of the fetus in his argument for the permissibility of abortion; Warren does the same. And so does Marquis in his argument against abortion. Thomson's pro-choice argument keeps the woman in the picture, but represents the fetus as a separate entity threatening to do the woman harm: In a series of thought experiments, she likens the fetus to an unconscious violinist the woman has to support for nine months; a burglar invading her house; and a people-seed that drifts in her window and takes root in the carpet. The conclusion we're supposed to draw from these thought experiments is that even if fetuses are persons, they are alien invaders with no claim on the woman's personal space.

Feminist bioethicists have reunited what nonfeminists have put asunder: They insist, like real estate agents, on the importance of location, location, location. A fetus grows only inside a woman's body, and the woman is purposefully and creatively engaged in its gestation. Human pregnancy is an *activity*, no more purely biological than any other human activity. Humans obey the laws of nature, but they improve on them, ordering and shaping what they find in the natural world through their own intentional, creative efforts. Out of the biological phenomenon of hunger, for example, they create dinner parties. Out of the upsurge of hormones that mark adolescence, they create coming-of-age rituals. So too with pregnancy. A pregnant woman is not just the "maternal background," but also an active participant in the process of bringing a new human into the world, starting from a fetus that is the flesh of her flesh, around which she weaves meaning. If she feels it as an intrusion she may figuratively push it away, distancing herself from it and rejecting the process in which she participates. Or she may embrace it lovingly from the beginning, imagining its future and establishing with it one of the most important relationships that will ultimately call it into personhood.

Unlike the prospective father or the grandparents or the bioethicists or the lawmakers, whose perspective on the pregnancy is an external one, the pregnant woman knows and experiences her body from her own inner perspective, from what the philosopher Thomas Nagel (1986) calls the internal point of view (113–14). This is the perspective, Nagel says, that lets us feel that we are the authors of our own actions—that we are agents rather than patients acted upon from the outside by biological, psychological, and social forces.

The pregnancy is part of the pregnant woman's inner perspective whether or not she wants to be pregnant. If the pregnancy is unwanted, the woman might feel alienated from herself, experiencing her state as an external fact that has nothing to do with who she is. But a feature can be both central and something you distance yourself from—think of a very beautiful woman who hates her beauty because it attracts people to her for the wrong reasons. Your pregnancy is a part of you in a way it can't be for other people, motivating you to orient yourself toward it or take action to stop it that's different from the motivations of those looking on from the outside.

This point about perspective is important because it takes women's experiences seriously: By weaving meaning around the natural biological process of pregnancy, the woman creates not just a human being but also a person with whom she is intimately connected. Her experience of pregnancy, however, doesn't yet provide an adequate basis for forming a moral judgment about the permissibility or otherwise of abortion. To get that, we have to add to it another feature of women's experience: the experience of gender as power over women. Gender sets up norms of subservience for women, and because gender is successful, the norms it establishes are firmly entrenched in actual social practices and institutions.

Who and what are women supposed to serve? The interests of powerful men, but also (and not coincidentally) the interests of religious institutions, business, the legal system, the health care delivery system, educational establishments, and the state. It is in the interest of these institutions to benefit from human reproduction without having to take responsibility for the ensuing children, and because the institutions wield considerable power, they have created office and factory spaces, work schedules, economic arrangements, patterns of living, and norms for behavior that promote this interest by forcing child care to take place elsewhere, off the premises. Gender provides the required army of servants needed to look after children, via the mechanism of a gendered division of labor that assigns a grossly disproportionate amount of the exhausting, demanding, self-sacrificing, and socially unrecognized work of reproducing and caring for children to women.

Combine the point about taking women's experience of pregnancy seriously with the point about the oppressive forces requiring women to serve the interests of others, and the argument over abortion becomes an argument about whether women themselves or a society that oppresses them should have control over women's bodies. Should pregnant women be forced to do the creative work of pregnancy, birthgiving, and child rearing, or should they have the power to control their bodies by putting a halt to the process of bringing a child into being? For people who enjoy a great deal of control in their lives, insisting on control can be unseemly and ungracious. For people who are routinely expected to sacrifice themselves for the good of those who don't have their interests at heart, control becomes pretty important. Under conditions of oppression, then, a strong argument can be made for leaving the decision whether to continue a pregnancy to the woman whose pregnancy it is.

This is not to say, of course, that any time a woman chooses to end a pregnancy she is doing the right thing. Her motives might be uncaring, disrespectful of the hopes and desires of her partner, frivolous, or self-hating. Because pregnancies set in train the reproduction of persons, they are morally valuable, so ending them is always a morally serious matter. But—and this is a big but—in a society where women are expected to be subservient and their bodily integrity is routinely violated by coerced sex, there is good reason to think that the *decision* must be theirs even if *what* they decide is all wrong.

Allocation of Health Care Resources

Whether we are talking about intensive care unit beds, kidneys for transplantation, mammograms, high blood pressure medication, or community-based mental health programs, the supply of health care resources always falls short of the demand. Demand, after all, is in principle unlimited, while health care resources are not. It follows, then, that in any society, health care resources have to be distributed according to some sort of system. The system we use in the United States is so patchwork that it's hard to see it as a system at all, but for everybody under the age of 65, it's pretty much based on the ability to pay, and even for the elderly, there is no guaranteed coverage for long-term care.

If bioethicists, whether feminist or not, agree on nothing else, they agree that the existing non-system is seriously unjust. Let me rehearse the statistics one more time: In 2004, health care spending in the United States reached $1.8 trillion, which amounts to 15.5 percent of the gross domestic product, which is more than the United States spends on defense and education combined. At the same time, some 44 million people (15.2 percent of the population) have no health care insurance at all, while another 60 million or so are badly underinsured. Clearly, some people are receiving lavish amounts of health care while others are going without. And this is a problem requiring feminist attention because the inequality of access to care is *gendered*—a fact that has escaped the attention of most nonfeminist bioethicists.

One way in which gender operates here is that women in their mid-forties or older are considerably less likely than men of the same age to have health insurance, either because they are more often part-time employees or because their coverage depended on their husbands and ceased when they were widowed or divorced. Because access to care is tied to employment, and even today the economics of marriage far more often dictate that wives must accommodate themselves to their husbands' careers than the other way around, the end of a marriage tends not only to impoverish women but to leave them uninsured. Lesbian and gay couples are in an even worse plight, because in most of the United States they may not marry and so are denied spousal health benefits. If they are underinsured and then fall seriously ill, no insurer will sell them additional coverage and their partner's insurer won't cover them either.

Second, the formal, professional health care delivery system is heavily dependent on the informal care given by families, and because of the gendered division of labor, roughly 80 percent of the 26 million family caregivers in the United States are women. This means that when HMOs or other health care institutions cut costs by shortening hospital stays, those costs are shifted to the women who provide the patient care that is still needed at home. The data gathered by the sociologist Elaine M. Brody indicate that while women want the men in the family to assume equal responsibility for care, men don't do it, though they're willing to provide financial help. A daughter says, "My two brothers and I are all busy lawyers. But when my mother got sick—she lives in another state—my brothers just assumed that I would be the one to fly out to her. And you know something? I did it." Similarly, when an elderly parent has no daughter, the obligation to give care falls on the daughter-in-law rather than the son. Said one woman, apparently without irony, when asked how *she* came to be her mother-in-law's caregiver, "My husband has two brothers, but he was always the one in the family who took the most responsibility" (quoted in Brody 1990, 80–82).

A third way in which the allocation of health care resources is gendered is that while women receive overall more professional health care than men, men receive considerably more of the expensive, high-tech care. Women between the ages of 46 and 60 are only half as likely to receive a kidney transplant as men of the same age, for example, while men are 6.5 times as likely to be referred for cardiac catheterization—a prerequisite for coronary bypass surgery—than women, even though men are only three times as likely to have coronary heart disease. The reason for these discrepancies is likely an economic one. If altering their work schedules to accommodate, say, three sessions a week on a kidney dialysis machine is more difficult for men than for women because men are more indispensable at work, then there will be corporate and other social pressures to transplant men over women. By the same token, if a man's financial contribution to the family is considerably larger than that of his wife (who has cut back her hours so that she can care for their children and the grandmother who can no longer live on her own), and if coronary bypass surgery is a more efficient and immediate solution to heart disease than drug therapy, bypass surgery will be considered as more crucial for him than for her.

And finally, a form of resource allocation that could be called "rationing by ordeal" is far more typical of women's experience than men's, simply because a greater proportion of women than men live below the poverty level—especially if they are single women with dependent children. Here is an example of how this kind of rationing works. A thirty-year-old sharecropper with three children, living in South Georgia, discovers she is pregnant. Her care is paid for by Medicaid, but her baby will have to be delivered in Waycross, fifty miles away, where the nearest hospital is located. To find a physician who will accept Medicaid patients, the sharecropper, who has no car or telephone, has to wait for a day when her brother-in-law can take her into town in his pickup, since the Greyhound bus no longer runs past her house. On the third try she finds a doctor who will care for her and she makes an appointment to see him in five weeks, his earliest available opening. When the day comes, her sister, who cared for her toddler and her four-year-old the last time, has hurt her back and can't look after the children, so the sharecropper brings them along. She waits for three hours to see the doctor, whose waiting room is badly overcrowded. The toddler is fractious. The four-year-old has nothing to do and picks fights with his sister. The doctor tells her she is anemic and that her baby could be born underweight if her vaginal infection doesn't clear up. He would like to see her again in two weeks. She and the children must then wait another two hours for her brother-in-law to finish his business before they can all go home. She can't face another day like this and misses her next appointment, thereby slightly relieving the overcrowding in the doctor's waiting room.

What sort of recommendations might feminist bioethicists make to the lawmakers who are in a position to fix the flaws like these that riddle our health care system? First, along with nonfeminist bioethicists, they would urge that health coverage be uncoupled from employment, since the disadvantages of the employment-linked system fall most heavily on women and poor men. They would replace that system with one that offers universal access to health care, in the form of either a national health service or a national system of insurance, pointing out that the United States is the only economically developed country in the world that doesn't provide access to health care for everyone. All the other developed countries regard health care as every person's right, and they manage to provide it even though they spend proportionately *less* money on health care than the United States does.

Second, feminist bioethicists might suggest that policy makers focus on outcomes rather than services. If, for example, there were a proven correlation between dropping out of school and bad health, a feminist system of health care would expend money and effort on keeping adolescents in school. There *is* a correlation between homelessness and bad health: When a family can no longer afford to pay rent, older children run away from their parents, younger children aren't fed properly, and the stress of homelessness produces heavy drinking, clinical depression, and chronic illness. So feminists might allocate resources for rent subsidies as a means of preventing the medical problems of homelessness.

This second point is important. Feminist bioethicists wouldn't put all the health care dollars in one pot and all the social service dollars in another. Because feminists tend to keep an eye on the big picture, where race, gender, class, and other abusive power systems form complicated interactions that affect all kinds of social practices, they're skeptical of the watertight compartments that are popularly erected among those practices. If justice in health care resource allocation is to be achieved, those walls, along with all the other walls that unfairly exclude or unfairly contain, will have to come down.

For Further Reading

Beauchamp, Tom L., and James F. Childress. 2001. *Principles of Biomedical Ethics*. 5th ed. New York: Oxford University Press.

Brody, Elaine M. 1990. *Women in the Middle: Their Parent-Care Years*. New York: Springer.

Buchanan, Allen E., and Dan W. Brock. 1989. *Deciding for Others: The Ethics of Surrogate Decision Making*. New York: Cambridge University Press.

Buchanan, Allen, Dan W. Brock, Norman Daniels, and Dan Wikler. 2000. *From Chance to Choice: Genetics and Justice*. New York: Cambridge University Press.

Case Study. 2002. "Mother and Son." *Hastings Center Report* 32 (5): 11.

Elliott, Carl. 2001. "Throwing a Bone to the Watchdog." *Hastings Center Report* 31 (2): 9–12.

Mahowald, Mary. 1996. "On Treatment of Myopia: Feminist Standpoint Theory and Bioethics." Pp. 95–115 in *Feminism and Bioethics: Beyond Reproduction*. Ed. Susan M. Wolf. New York: Oxford.

Miles, Steven H., and Alison August. 1990. "Courts, Gender, and the Right to Die." *Journal of Law, Medicine, and Health Care* 18: 85–95.

Nagel, Thomas. 1986. *The View from Nowhere*. New York: Oxford University Press.

Parks, Jennifer. 2000. "Why Gender Matters in the Euthanasia Debate." *Hastings Center Report* 30 (1): 30–36.

Petchesky, Rosalind Pollack. 1987. "Fetal Images: The Power of Visual Culture in the Politics of Reproduction." *Feminist Studies* 13 (2): 263–88.

Rachels, James. 1975. "Active and Passive Euthanasia." *New England Journal of Medicine* 292, no. 2 (January 9): 78–80.

Sherwin, Susan. 1992. *No Longer Patient: Feminist Ethics and Health Care*. Philadelphia: Temple University Press.

Wolf, Susan M. 1996. "Gender, Feminism, and Death: Physician-Assisted Suicide and Euthanasia." Pp. 282–317 in *Feminism and Bioethics: Beyond Reproduction*. Ed. Susan M. Wolf. New York: Oxford.

CHAPTER

7

Violence

I was listening to a report on National Public Radio the other day about a war being waged on the other side of the world, when it suddenly occurred to me that all the voices I was hearing, whether of combatants, politicians, or analysts, were *men's* voices. It's hardly news that the overwhelming majority of people who make and fight wars are men, but stay with that thought for a moment. Don't take it for granted (as the philosopher Ludwig Wittgenstein might say), but let it *strike* you that war—a concerted, violent response to political differences—is waged largely by men. Now let it strike you that over 90 percent of people convicted of violent crime are men. That almost all rapists are men. That over 90 percent of domestic violence is inflicted by men.

Once you've thought all that over, consider the images and stories circulating through our culture—what I called master narratives in Chapter Three—that portray violence as manly. Pick any movie starring Bruce Willis, Vin Diesel, or The Rock, and you get the message that real men aren't supposed to let anybody push them around. Nor, when real men are angry, are they supposed to sit down and talk about it—they're supposed to do something, and this typically means killing the bad guys. The fact that action heroes are idealized fantasy-figures rather than actual people is precisely the point: *Ideal* men are violent. They're the men that little boys (and big ones) want to be when they grow up. To say that violence is gendered, then, isn't just to say that many more men than women commit acts of violence, though it certainly is to say at least this much. That violence is gendered also means that it is a *norm* for men. It's how men are supposed to be, and in many arenas of life they get rewarded for being it.

The gendered nature of violence makes it a central topic for feminist ethics. In this chapter I'll focus on three forms of violence that are socially condemned (though often they go unpunished), because with these forms it's easier to see how violence operates as a pressive force that keeps women subservient to men. I'll start with rape, then move to rape in war, and bring it back home with a look at domestic violence.

7.1. Rape

A frequently heard rape statistic is that one out of every four women in the United States will be sexually assaulted in her lifetime, though the Coalition Educating about Sexual Endangerment claims that the figure is actually one in three. The other widely quoted statistic is that every two minutes, somewhere in the U.S. a woman is raped, though Safe Daughters more than doubles this figure: They say it's once every 45 seconds. An Abuse, Rape, and Domestic Violence Aid and Resource Collection (AARDVARC) reports that the incidence of forcible rape increased 4 percent in 2002, while the Rape, Abuse, and Incest National Network (RAINN) claims that since 1993, rape and sexual assault has fallen by half.

You see the problem. Rape statistics are notoriously unreliable, and as a consequence, no one is sure exactly how much rape goes on and whether the figures are getting better or worse in any given year. This is not to say that generalizations are impossible: The figures gathered by government agencies and social scientists demonstrate plainly that significant numbers of men rape women, and while fewer men rape other men and children, those rapes too are widespread.

A reason frequently given for the lack of reliable information about the incidence of rape is that it often goes unreported. The FBI estimates that only 37 percent of all rapes are brought to the attention of the police. Other estimates are even lower, ranging from the U.S. Department of Justice's 26 percent to the Coalition Educating about Sexual Endangerment's 16 percent. Underreporting is often attributed to the victim's fear that she will be blamed, that the rape will stigmatize her, or that her rapist will punish her for telling. Equally important, though, might be two other factors.

First, girls between the ages of 16 and 24 are about three times as likely to be raped as older women, but because most of them are raped by their dates, boyfriends, or other guys they know, they very often—over 70 percent on some college campuses—don't think of it as rape. Second, according to a 1993 Senate Judiciary Report (the most recent data we have), 84 percent of the rapes that *are* reported don't result in a conviction, and almost half of convicted rapists serve less than a year in prison. So victims who do go to the police and press charges are very likely to suffer the ordeal of testimony and humiliating cross-examination, only to see their assailants walk away.

These last two considerations are connected, in that they both rest on what many feminists argue are defective theories of rape. These theories are of two kinds, one having to do with who counts as a rapist, and the other having to do with why rape is morally and legally wrong. As to who counts as a rapist, if you believe that rapists are strange men lurking in alleyways, then what your date's buddies did to you won't get registered as rape, even though it traumatizes, frightens, and humiliates you. Instead, you'll probably think the party got out of hand, or you were drunk and led them on, or they were just blowing off steam.

As to the moral and legal wrongness of rape, the feminist philosopher Ann Cahill has usefully divided theories about this into three kinds, which I will call property, consent, and abusive group relations theories.

Property Theories

According to the traditional Western understanding of rape, women had a legal identity only as it was derived from the fathers, husbands, or brothers under whose protection they lived. In his *Commentaries on the Laws of England* (1765) the noted jurist William Blackstone put it this way: "By marriage, the husband and the wife are one person in law; that is, the very being or legal existence of the woman is suspended during the marriage, or at least is incorporated and consolidated into that of the husband" (quoted in Cahill 2001, 17). Since a woman had no independent standing under the law, rape wasn't seen as an offense against her.

Instead, it was an offense against her male relatives or guardians, who were entitled to her chastity so that she could be married well or, if already married, produce children who were surely her husband's. On this view of rape, a woman was a special kind of property and rape was the unlawful use of that property. In some cases, particularly if the victim was a virgin, her rape was considered the theft of something valuable and irreplaceable for which her father was owed compensation.

Consent Theories

Times change and so do laws. In most economically developed nations, property theories of rape have been replaced by consent ones. As consent theories have it, women have the same rights under the law that men do, so rape should be understood as a violation of those individually held rights. It's a type of battery, more or less equal to any other kind of bodily assault, and as the legal definition of *battery* is "unconsented touching," whether a woman has been raped hinges on the question of whether she has consented to that particular sexual encounter. Statutory rape—the rape of a minor—counts as rape on consent views precisely because the victim is deemed too young to give free and informed consent, and a rapist's best legal defense on these views is to show that the woman agreed to have sex with him.

A number of feminist theories of rape developed in the 1970s belong in the consent camp. So, for example, the radical lesbian feminists Carolyn Shafer and Marilyn Frye wrote: "Since we share the public view that rape is morally wrong and gravely so, and since we would not want to say that there is anything morally wrong with sexual intercourse per se, we conclude that the wrongness of rape rests with the matter of the woman's consent" (quoted in Cahill 2001, 169). Similarly, the political theorist Carole Pateman assumes that the wrongness of rape hinges on consent, but she goes on to argue that when a "'naturally' superior, active, and sexually aggressive male makes an initiative, or offers a contract, to which a 'naturally' subordinate, passive woman 'consents,'" there can be no egalitarian sexual relationship, and therefore, paradoxically, this is a situation that is structurally opposed to the possibility of consent (quoted in Cahill 2001, 164). If Pateman is right about this, then *all* heterosexual intercourse is rape—a view, famously held by the feminist legal theorist Catharine MacKinnon, that goes considerably beyond most consent theories. Like other consent theorists, though, Pateman thinks that if genuine equality existed, consent would serve as the dividing line between sexual encounters that are right and sexual encounters that are wrong.

Consent-based theories inform current rape laws, but there's a practical problem with how consent operates here that goes some distance toward explaining why so few rapists are punished. What I mean is this: Under U.S. law, the accused is innocent until proven guilty, so the burden of proof is on the accuser. If, say, Jack is charged with stealing Jill's wallet, Jill has to prove that it was her wallet and that Jack took it. The standard of evidence she has to meet is quite high: She has to prove his guilt "beyond a reasonable doubt." But she doesn't, typically, have to prove at the same time that she didn't consent to his taking the wallet: It's assumed that she didn't, unless he can prove she did. And it doesn't matter if she was drunk and left the wallet lying on the bar—that's irrelevant to the question of whether he took something that didn't belong to him. So, in cases of theft, the presumption is that no consent was given.

With rape it's different. There, Jill has to prove not only that Jack took *her,* but that she didn't consent to being taken. And this amounts to having to prove a negative, which is generally not easy to do, and if she can't, *she* is presumed guilty of making a false accusation. How can we account for this difference between rape and theft as consent theories understand them?

The difference, I think, has to do with the conditions under which rape and theft occur. Wallets are stolen regularly by perfect strangers—by pickpockets or other people with whom the victim isn't in any special relationship of trust. There, it makes a certain amount of sense to presume that no consent was given. It's only within the small circle of people we trust with our wallets that "you gave it to me" could count as a reasonable defense against an accusation of theft. Rape, on the other hand, is often inflicted by someone with whom the victim *is* in a special trust relationship:

He is her friend, her date, her father or brother. Within that kind of relationship, though she might trust him with her wallet, it doesn't follow that she also trusts him with her body, her dignity, her physical and emotional nakedness, her vulnerability to disease and perhaps unwanted pregnancy. In fact, she may trust him precisely *not* to think that he has access to her body, so that when he rapes her, he betrays that very trust.

Consent theories of rape are closely connected to the dominant moral theories we examined in Chapter Four. Like them, they tend to treat all human relationships as if they consisted of impersonal interactions between self-sufficient individuals who are in a position to bargain as equals for their own best interests—relationships that, as we've seen before, occupy the public sphere. These are, for the most part, relationships among strangers, and it's here that consent works properly: The default assumption is that I didn't consent to your taking my wallet. The reason that consent theories of rape don't work as well as consent theories of theft, though, is that sexual relations don't typically take place in the public sphere, and the theories aren't equipped to say much of anything about what goes on in private. In relationships of intimacy, the interactions aren't impersonal: My boyfriend isn't replaceable by any other similarly situated individual, and I shouldn't want him to act toward me only as he'd be willing to act toward all other women. I'm supposed to care about his best interests in addition to my own, and he's supposed to favor me over other women in my position.

Consent theories of rape aren't well equipped to capture either the personal nature of sexual intimacy or the special kind of trust that underlies a morally sound sexual relationship. They don't have the resources for conceptualizing the betrayal of trust among friends or family, or the exploitation of bodily and emotional vulnerability. So, while these theories do pick up on the moral importance of consent in a sexual relationship, they miss all the other morally significant features of the private and personal context in which many rapes take place. As a result, they mistake the trust relationship of the private sphere for presumed consent, which means the burden is on the victim to show she *didn't* consent.

What counts as proof of lack of consent is complicated by the variety of relationships—including some pretty casual ones—in which many people have enjoyable sex. For an illustration of how uncertain the standard of proof can be, consider the case of Kobe Bryant, the Los Angeles Lakers basketball star accused of raping a nineteen-year-old woman in his hotel room at a Vail-area resort where she worked. The bruises found on the woman during a hospital examination were admitted into evidence, but the defense lawyers suggested that the woman had multiple sexual partners in the days surrounding her encounter with Bryant, including sex with someone after the alleged attack, and they argued that the bruises could have been inflicted by any of these other men. The woman denied the defense's suggestion, but the fact that the lawyers made a point of her sexual activity *after* Bryant allegedly raped her reveals how differently consent operates in cases of rape as opposed to cases of theft. It's hard to see how the fact that Jill gave money to a friend just after Jack took her wallet has any bearing on Jack's guilt. The really striking thing, though, is the defense's assumption that any other sexual encounter might just as easily have been the cause of her injuries, as if force to the point of bruising were a normal thing that happens to women during sex. (This is an instance of Lindemann's ad hoc rule Number 74: You will never fail to be amazed by what some people can take for granted.)

Abusive Group Relations Theories

One problem, then, with consent-based theories of rape is that they don't have the resources to conceptualize special relationships of trust as anything other than consent. But an even bigger problem is that the theories, in treating rape as a gender-neutral violation of individual rights, tend to peel off its sexual aspects, likening it to battery, assault, and (as I just did) robbery. The advantage of conceptualizing rape as a particularly nasty way to slug someone is that it foregrounds the violence of the act rather than the victim's voluptuousness, thereby undercutting the "she was so sexy I couldn't help myself" defense. But let's consider whether assaulting someone with a penis really *is* no different from assaulting her with a baseball bat.

An assault with a bat, bottle, or fist is an assault not only on the victim's body but also his mind. It shatters his sense of security and perhaps his dignity, inflicting emotional scars as well as physical ones. Like robbery, battery can leave the victim feeling invaded, personally violated, or sullied by the crime. But neither robbery nor battery is a direct attack on the victim's sexuality, and that's an important difference. Unlike the average robber or mugger, the rapist is sexually aroused: He gets an erection and often has an orgasm. By violating the victim not only in her body and her mind but also in her sexuality, the rapist inflicts damage that goes beyond other offenses against persons—he damages her identity. Many victims report that in the aftermath of rape, having sex causes them to relive the experience all over again, so that resuming ordinary sexual relations is impossible for months or even years later.

While an attack with a penis is clearly an attack with a sexualized weapon, other weapons can be sexualized as well. Shoving a bottle up a vagina is not simple battery but rape, as was shoving a plunger handle up the rectum and into the mouth of Abner Louima, an innocent man tortured by New York police officers inside the Seventieth Precinct office in Brooklyn on 9 August 1997. As is made vividly clear by the infamous photographs of Iraqi prisoners in sexually humiliating poses taken at Abu Ghraib prison by their military jailers, violating people's sexuality is a particularly vicious way of degrading them.

Rape, then, is *sexualized* violence, but it is also the expression of one group's contempt for another. In the Abner Louima case the contempt was racial: The white New York police officers didn't have anything against him personally—he was just a handy target for their attitude toward black men as a group. In the far more common cases of heterosexual rape, the perpetrator likewise uses the victim as a stand-in for the group, here, for women in general. The rapist, like the robber or mugger, forces his will on the victim, refusing to recognize that she is a morally valuable person in her own right, with her own intentions, thoughts, feelings, and wishes. Unlike the robber or mugger, though, the rapist chooses his victim because his social group stands in an abusive relation to hers, and according to the norms that are built into the relation, women *as a group* exist to serve men. What this means sexually speaking is that men are supposed to be powerful and dominant; women are supposed to be passive and compliant. Men are supposed to take pleasure; women are supposed to give it. Strip away the veneer of chivalry that hides the uglier norms of this power relation from view, and women are basically vaginas or other orifices where men are entitled to put their penises.

On theories of rape that take abusive power relations between men and women, blacks and whites, and other social groups into account, rape isn't merely an offense against an individual. It is also a way of degrading a group that is already less powerful than the group to which the rapist belongs, or, in some cases, of challenging a dominant group—as when a man living in poverty rapes a woman living on Park Avenue.

As I remarked in Chapter One, gender is a norm, not a fact about people, and because it's an effective norm, it creates the differences between men and women that keep it going. As Cahill (2001) argues, the gendered act of rape constructs male sexuality "such that it constitutes a way of imposing harm, pain, and powerlessness. It . . . constructs female sexuality in terms of passivity, victimhood, and lack of agency" (27). In creating and maintaining these differences between men's and women's sexuality, rape functions as what Claudia Card (2002) calls "a domestic protection racket" (128). The norms of passivity, victimhood, and lack of agency that rape imposes on women force them to seek protection from their more powerful counterparts. So men in essence offer women a deal: They will keep other men from raping them, in exchange for sexual services and for doing the tasks (such as giving care) that men themselves don't want to do. This is an offer that too many women literally can't refuse.

Notice that the protection racket *subjugates* women. In addition to pressing women into performing services for men, fear of rape prompts women to protect their bodies by restricting their scope of movement, and this is a posture of submission. The feminist philosopher Sandra Lee Bartky (1990) puts it this way: "Women's space is not a field in which her bodily intentionality can be freely realized but an enclosure in which she feels herself positioned and by which she is confined" (67). This enclosure is often imposed on women by others. At the University of Tennessee–Knoxville, for example, while fraternities are housed off campus in spacious and elegant buildings, sororities are not permitted off campus but instead are housed in utilitarian dormitories. The arrangement is justified on the grounds that it offers the women better protection—it's for their own good, supposedly, to be kept under heightened surveillance. While on-campus housing may indeed contribute to women's safety, it also preserves their subordinate status vis-à-vis men: They get the inferior housing.

If, as I argue, rape is a sexualized form of violence both arising out of and sustaining abusive group relations, what can be done to stop it? In the 1980s and 90s, a widespread approach to rape prevention was that of risk management. Private companies supplied women with gadgets, alarms, and pepper spray, while workplaces and colleges enticed women to attend sexual assault prevention workshops with advertisements like this one:

> A woman is raped every five minutes in this country. Three out of four American women will be violently, physically, or sexually assaulted in their lifetimes. These statistics speak to the need for women to learn how to lead safer and more secure lives. This informative and participatory workshop will discuss sexual issues as well as include tips on how to be safer at home, in your car, and in public. This workshop is designed for women. This is not a self-defense class. (quoted in Hall 2004, 6)

In November 1995 the American Medical Association issued a statement to the effect that sexual assault "claims a victim every 45 seconds" and cautioning that patients might be "push[ed] into the shadows, afraid to step forward and seek help from their physicians." While the AMA statement was not directed specifically at women but at their doctors, it was titled "the silent violent epidemic," thereby implying that rape was a kind of virus a woman might catch if she weren't careful. On many campuses, large signs posted by campus security urge women never to walk by themselves at night and to stay in lighted areas. Also, many women are taught to hold their car keys in their hand while walking through a parking lot on the way to their car, and to lock their doors and windows.

What the sorority housing strategy, rape safety marketing, rape prevention workshops, talk of rape as an epidemic, and large signs cautioning women to watch out all have in common is that no actual rapists are visible here. They are erased through the use of the passive voice ("A woman is raped every five minutes." By what?) or through scary statistics about how often rape "occurs"—as if it were a random force of nature, like lightning or smallpox. With the rapist pushed unobtrusively out of the picture, the responsibility to do something about rape falls squarely on the women who are endangered, rather than on those who have the authority to impose sanctions on their attackers. For sanctions, an actual perpetrator is required; for prevention, no such person is necessary.

As the cultural theorist Rachel Hall points out, the risk management approach to rape not only targets women inappropriately as the site for interventions against rape, it also positions women as abstract victims, thereby justifying endless intrusions into actual women's lives "for their own good." Her solution is to urge those working in the anti-rape movement to concentrate on three tasks: shifting the focus of interventions against rape from women to men, dismissing the abstract figure of Woman as victim, and challenging the images and stories of rape that make it appear to be a random force of nature (Hall 2004, 15). If, however, rape is best understood as the product of abusive group relations, it's a political problem and therefore not one that can be solved by anti-rape workers alone. What's needed in addition is concerted political action aimed at dismantling the power arrangement that subordinates women to men.

One strategy for dismantling that arrangement might be to shift the burden of proof so that it falls on the dominant group rather than the subordinated one. The victim would still have to establish that this particular man had sex with her, but the burden would be on the man in question to show that the sexual encounter was with her consent.

That would make men think twice before having sex with anyone, whether male or female, which might not be such a bad thing. And it would protect rape victims from the hostility, contempt, and humiliation that friends, family, perfect strangers, and the courts too often inflict on them under the current system.

7.2. Rape in War

Among the many violent practices that are carried out in wartime, two in particular involve rape. The first consists of enslaving women and girls for sexual service. The most highly publicized example is probably the "comfort women" who were forced to service Japanese soldiers—sometimes as many as thirty a day—in "comfort stations" throughout the Far East during the Second World War. As Card (2002) explains, the purpose of wartime sexual slavery is recreation for soldiers and officers, and after the infamous Rape of Nanking, comfort stations were further justified on the grounds that these men would otherwise rape indiscriminately and thereby stiffen resistance movements within occupied territories (119). At the end of the war, when many Japanese soldiers opted for suicide over capture, some first raked houses full of comfort women with machine-gun fire to prevent enemy troops from freeing them. Some women survived, and a handful of these recently came forward pressing claims for compensation. But many survivors say they want nothing to do with compensation, feeling that though they were not prostitutes then, they would be if they accepted money now.

The second wartime practice of rape—as an instrument of war—has a different purpose. The sexual violence inflicted on Croatian, Serbian, and Tutsi women in the 1990s wars in Bosnia-Herzegovina and Rwanda, or Sudanese women in Darfur in the early 2000s, is not aimed at providing recreation for soldiers and officers, though the pleasure they take in it might explain their willingness to do it. Rather, the aim of rape as an instrument of war is to intimidate and demoralize the enemy, to disrupt families and communities by forcing women into pregnancies that alter the ethnic identity of the next generation, and to establish the dominance of the conquering tribe or nation. The psychologist Libby Tata Arcel offers a useful definition of rape as a weapon of war:

> Forcible penetration or near-penetration (vaginal, rectal, oral) of a woman's body openings by body parts of or any instruments used by a person in official capacity during armed conflict. . . . Rape includes cases where a woman is coerced to exchange sexual favors for certain entitlements for herself or her family (food, necessary papers, health services). (quoted in Schott 2003, 101–102)

Here, the woman raped is a secondary target, used to humiliate and manipulate the primary targets: her husband, father, and brothers. She's a throwaway item, a means of exacting submission and compliance from the men of her community. But she also serves a symbolic function. In many cultures the mother's body is identified with the earth, the "land" in its political sense of a territory, kingdom, or nation: To rape the kingdom's women is to rape the kingdom. Just as in times of peace women's fertility is a symbol of nation building, ensuring new citizens to make the nation strong, so in times of war her violated body symbolizes a violated future, a land polluted not only now but for the next generation as well.

This symbolism, however, often backfires onto the actual women who have been victimized by rape in war. The very fact that they have been raped typically brings shame on them, especially if the rape issues in a child. After the 1990 wars in Rwanda, many women known to have been raped were expelled from their communities, forced to live outside the protection of their families. This also occurred in the case of Bengali women raped by Pakistani soldiers in 1971, and it is occurring now in Darfur, Uganda, and other war-torn parts of the world. The women themselves frequently experience profound humiliation, a sense of "homelessness" in their own bodies (Schott 2003, 109), and a precarious existence on the fringes of their society.

If the purpose of rape as an instrument of war is to demoralize the enemy, disrupt communal and familial bonds, and establish dominance, the question arises as to why *rape* is particularly suited to achieving these goals. Wouldn't plundering and burning, carpet bombing, destroying local industries, shooting, torturing, and terrorizing do the job just as well? The answer, of course, is that these other means are often employed in wartime. But as Card (2002) explains, "Because of its sexual character, rape in a patriarchal culture has a special potential to drive a wedge between family members and to carry the expression of the perpetrator's dominance into future generations. And the act of rape itself is a multicultural symbol of domination" (129).

Card suggests that rape in war might occur less frequently if women entered the military in equal numbers with men—if well-trained women fought side by side with men under the command of well-trained women officers. Under those conditions, she believes, rape would be unlikely to retain its symbolism of dominance, so there would be less incentive for men to do it. Sara Ruddick thinks this solution is ultimately self-defeating, because it leaves in place a way of thinking that glorifies war—a mindset in which dominance is the point and violence is awarded medals. I share Ruddick's worry, even if, as Card (2002) proposes, women participated in the military "in the spirit of conscientious draftees without succumbing to martial values" (131). And if, as I've been arguing, rape in war, like rape in peacetime, is a product of abusive group relations between men and women, it isn't likely to stop unless the social and political institutions maintaining those abusive relations are restructured to be hospitable to women.

7.3. Domestic Violence

As with statistics on the incidence of rape, reliable statistics on domestic violence are hard to come by, because so much of it goes unreported. In the early 1990s the FBI estimated that 90 percent of domestic violence never comes to the attention of the police. If a 1994 report issued by the U.S. Department of Justice's Bureau of Justice Statistics is to be believed, however, domestic violence is highly gendered: Ninety-two percent of it is inflicted by men on women. In 1998 the Department of Justice issued another arresting statistic: While women are less likely than men to be victims of violent crimes overall, they are five to eight times more likely than men to be victimized by an intimate partner. Of those who reported being physically assaulted since the age of eighteen, 76 percent were attacked by a date, boyfriend, cohabitating partner, or current or former husband. According to a report issued in 2001 by the American Institute on Domestic Violence:

- Every 9 seconds a woman is beaten in the United States.
- Between 3 and 4 million women are battered each year.
- Eighty-five to 95 percent of all domestic violence victims are girls and women.
- Women aged 20–40 endure the highest rates of domestic violence.
- Domestic violence is the leading cause of injury to women.
- Homicide is the leading cause of death to women in the workplace.

And one last statistic: In January 2004 the president-elect of the American Medical Association reported that the most common reason for a woman between the ages of 15 and 44 to go to the emergency room is that she was battered at home.

Physical violence isn't the only form of abuse dished out by husbands, partners, and boyfriends. Other kinds include *isolation,* which makes women dependent on their partners; *monopolization of perception,* which fixes women's attention on their immediate predicament to the exclusion of other stimuli; *inducing of debility and exhaustion,* which weakens women's ability to resist; *threats,* which produce anxiety and despair; *occasional indulgences,* which make women cooperative and grateful to their partners; *demonstration of omnipotence,* which produces the sense that resistance is futile; *degradation,* which makes capitulation less damaging to women's self-respect than resistance; and *enforcing trivial demands,* which develops the habit of compliance (Card 2002, 144–45).

These techniques, which work best when they form a pattern of behaviors extending over a period of time, have been dubbed "gaslighting," after the movie starring Ingrid

Bergman and Charles Boyer. In *Gaslight,* the Boyer character, who has murdered the Bergman character's aunt, marries the Bergman character so that he can steal the valuable jewels the aunt hid before she died. Bergman, of course, is unaware of his villainous intent and believes he truly loves her. To keep her from finding out what he is doing, Boyer uses many of the tactics listed above to dominate her and reduce her to bewildered helplessness. As the story unfolds, we see Bergman come to doubt her sanity, no longer trusting herself to get anything right, until she is almost totally dependent on her husband both physically and mentally.

Gaslighting techniques, by the way, aren't confined to the privacy of home: They are also the ones that Amnesty International identifies as those used by torturers in terrorist organizations. Yet, as the researchers on family violence Richard Gelles and Murray Straus observe, "The amount of money allocated to prevent and treat private violence and abuse is so small that it would be considered a rounding error in the Defense Department" (quoted in Wilkerson 1998, 128).

The lawyer Mindy Lazarus-Black spent eight months observing what happens when women who are victims of domestic violence take their batterers to court. Many women can't afford to hire their own lawyers, either because they live in poverty or because their partners withhold joint income from them as a way of controlling them. The women then have to rely on the services of a public defender, who usually has a staggering caseload and no support staff to gather evidence, such as medical records and emergency-room admissions, that would strengthen the case against the batterer. Lazarus-Black tells of one woman who did manage to hire a private attorney with funds she scraped together from her family. On the day of the hearing the attorney failed to appear—he simply forgot to show up. The judge waited for him impatiently and finally scolded the woman for not telling her lawyer where and when the hearing would take place, even though she *had* notified the lawyer and doing this is the court's responsibility in any case. The judge then set another date for three weeks later, leaving the woman without the order of protection she had been seeking. After enduring three more weeks of physical abuse, she returned to court, but because she was overcome with shame and her attorney had neglected to prepare her to testify, she minimized what her batterer had done to her, with the result that the judge threw the case out of court (Bartky 2004, 25–26).

It's quite common for victims of domestic abuse to feel shame and to downplay their injuries—consider what repeated, long-term violence and gaslighting by a person you love and trust can do to you. Domestic abusers take advantage of the special vulnerability that accompanies intimacy to break down the victim's self-respect, causing her to condone or excuse behavior that she wouldn't tolerate from anyone else and, in extreme cases, making her feel that she isn't worth anything except as his punching bag. It's hard to stand up for yourself when someone dear to you has broken your spirit as well as your bones, because you no longer believe you are worth standing up for. And if he hasn't broken your spirit, you still have every reason not to make matters worse for yourself by getting out of the relationship and reporting him to the police. According to Sandra Bartky (2004), "The woman is most at risk of murderous violence when she attempts to terminate the relationship or when she has succeeded, through divorce or legal separation, in actually leaving it" (29).

Domestic violence is too widespread to be explained as the actions of a few men who lose their tempers now and then. Like rape and sexual aggression in war, it's an expression of the abusive power system we have been calling gender. Judith Herman argues that this power system isn't merely *expressed*, but is actually *kept in place by* violence in the home: "The subordinate condition of women is maintained and enforced by the hidden violence of men. There is war between the sexes. Rape victims, battered women, and sexually abused children are its casualties" (quoted in Card 2002, 144).

And just as gender is enforced by domestic violence, so too domestic violence is supported by gender. Researchers frequently report that batterers' behavior is condoned and reinforced by their male friends. Lee H. Bowker, who studied one thousand survivors of domestic violence, found that "the more frequently a man socialized with his friends, the more severely and extensively he battered his wife." According to R. Emerson Dobash and Russell Dobash, "The woman's friends or relations are much more likely to intervene than the husband's" (quoted in Wilkerson 1998, 128).

Battered women's shelters are a help, though many more are needed. Mandatory reporting by police and physicians, mandatory arrest, better intervention and support services, and universal access to good health care would also be a help. At the end of the day, however, these are all stopgap measures. The problem of domestic violence, like the problem of other gendered forms of violence, can't ultimately be solved until abusive gender relations no longer exist. Nothing short of social transformation will do.

How would that social transformation get started? We could begin by challenging the morally dubious master narratives that idealize violent men. Master narratives of "manly" tough guys don't merely oppress women and glorify violence—they're untrue. How many men do you know who slap women around or use their fists to settle quarrels? If you are yourself a man, you probably don't behave that way either.

What we need here are *counterstories:* stories that resist these harmful master narratives and sets up a better ideal for boys and men to aim at. What would such counterstories look like? Writing about the inhabitants of the French village of Le Chambon, who hid many Jews from the Nazis during the Second World War, Phillip Hallie (1979) says: "*Lucid knowledge, awareness of the pain of others,* and *stubborn decision* dissipated for the Chambonnais the Night and Fog that inhabited the minds of so many people in Europe, and the world at large, in 1942" (104, my italics). These morally admirable and indeed heroic people opposed the violence that engulfed their world, and their values might be the very ones to inform our counterstories. Stories that portray men stubbornly resisting myths of monstrous villains and splendid warriors—and just as stubbornly standing up for their best judgment of what's right and good. Stories that portray men attentive to human misery and suffering—and equally attentive to the riches of the world that make life worth living. Stories that portray men clear eyed and clear headed—and just as lucidly aware of their own strengths and weaknesses as of the evils in the world. Nor need men be the only ones to tell these stories. Let's all be telling them, now and for the rest of our lives.

For Further Reading

Bartky, Sandra Lee. 1990. *Femininity and Domination: Studies in the Phenomenology of Oppression.* New York: Routledge.

———. 2004. "Intimidation." Pp. 19–31 in *Moral Psychology: Feminist Ethics and Social Theory.* Ed. Peggy DesAutels and Margaret Urban Walker. Lanham, MD: Rowman & Littlefield.

Brison, Susan J. 2002. *Aftermath: Violence and the Remaking of a Self.* Princeton: Princeton University Press.

Cahill, Ann. 2001. *Rethinking Rape.* Ithaca, NY: Cornell University Press.

Card, Claudia. 2002. *The Atrocity Paradigm: A Theory of Evil.* New York: Oxford University Press.

DesAutels, Peggy, and Margaret Urban Walker. 2004. *Moral Psychology: Feminist Ethics and Social Theory.* Lanham, MD: Rowman & Littlefield.

Hall, Rachel. 2004. "It Can Happen to You: Rape Prevention in the Age of Risk Management." *Hypatia* 19 (3): 1–19.

Hallie, Phillip. 1979. *Lest Innocent Blood Be Shed.* New York: Harper & Row.

Schott, Robin May. 2003. *Discovering Feminist Philosophy: Knowledge, Ethics, Politics.* Lanham, MD: Rowman & Littlefield.

Wilkerson, Abby L. 1998. *Diagnosis: Difference.* Ithaca, NY: Cornell University Press.

CHAPTER 8

Globalization and Cross-Cultural Judgments

We live in cosmopolitan times. Never before has the world seen such extensive and intense international trade and travel—a point brought home neatly by this description of a fairly recent royal catastrophe: "An English Princess with an Egyptian boyfriend uses a Norwegian mobile telephone, crashes in a French tunnel in a German car with a Dutch engine, driven by a Belgian driver who was high on Scottish whiskey, followed closely by Italian paparazzi on Japanese bicycles, treated by an American doctor, assisted by Filipino paramedical staff, using Brazilian medicines, dies!"

Systems of transcontinental exchange are as old as the Stone Age migrations out of Africa, the tribal conquests and displacements of Bronze Age Europe and Asia, the far-flung outposts of the Roman Empire, and the colonial period of Modern Europe. All such exchanges could, broadly speaking, be called globalization, but what sets the current system apart from older ones is that it integrates local and national markets into a single global economy, regulated since 1995 by the World Trade Organization (WTO) and administered by the International Monetary Fund (IMF) and the World Bank.

But what, you may ask, has globalization got to do with feminist ethics? Quite a lot. For one thing, in its current, neoliberal form (more on neoliberalism in a minute) it further impoverishes the poorest countries of the world and lines the pockets of the richest, joining forces with gender to intensify the oppression of women in debtor nations. For another, "women's work" has itself become globalized, often with disastrous consequences. Feminist ethics offers resources, first, for *describing* how gender and neoliberal globalization interact;

and second, for *assessing*, in moral terms, the damage inflicted on women in particular by the combination of these two abusive power systems. These tasks are arguably the most urgent ones confronting feminist ethics today.

8.1. The So-Called Southern Debt

Let's begin our ethical analysis of globalization by making a distinction between the global North and the global South. Roughly, as Alison M. Jaggar (2002) observes, the global North refers to the world's wealthiest, highly industrialized nations, most of which are in the northern hemisphere. The global South refers to poorer countries, many in the southern hemisphere, that depend mostly on agriculture, mining, and logging, while their manufacturing industries, if any, are typically owned by foreign investors. Northern states, whose indigenous populations tend to be light skinned, often have a history of colonizing others, while Southern states, whose indigenous people tend to be brown skinned, have often been colonized and continue to suffer from the aftereffects of colonization. Although the North–South distinction is a useful shorthand, it's important not to take it literally—Australia and New Zealand are Northern countries, for example.

According to Jaggar, in the 1970s, when interest rates were low, many Southern countries borrowed massively to finance their social and economic development. At the end of the decade, however, when interest rates rose sharply, most debtor nations had trouble paying the interest they owed. This resulted in a world debt crisis in the 1980s that threatened a collapse of the global economy. The IMF and the World Bank, fearing the worst, rescheduled many of the largest debts while simultaneously imposing structural adjustment policies as a condition for debt relief. Structural adjustment policies, as their name implies, adjust the structures of local economies so that they can be integrated into the global economic system, allowing debtor countries to earn enough foreign currency so that they can repay their debts. Typically, the policies require Southern countries to slash government spending on social projects and services, privatize state enterprises and deregulate industries, make natural resources available for commercial exploitation, produce cash crops and other goods for export, open their markets to foreign investors, and devalue local currencies so that the country's exports are relatively cheaper for other nations and imports are more expensive.

Structural adjustment policies have been wildly successful as far as the North is concerned, because they have guaranteed that an increasing proportion of Southern countries' resources go to servicing foreign debts. As far as the South is concerned, however, the policies have been a disaster. For one thing, the promotion of cash crops has encouraged Southern countries to become permanently dependent on Northern machines and fertilizers, thereby creating guaranteed markets for Northern manufactured goods. At the same time, the policies ensure a supply of cheap labor and cheap raw materials for Northern industries. The exchange is not an even one: Terms of trade for raw materials tend to be far less favorable than terms for manufactured products, so the North becomes richer and the South poorer.

Another problem with structural adjustment policies is that local economies don't always have the capital to compete successfully in global markets. In Central America, for example, popular supermarket chains owned by global corporations like the Dutch multinational Ahold and U.S.-based Wal-Mart buy only unblemished produce of a specified size and shape, but many local farmers lack the expertise as well as the money to invest in the modern greenhouses, pest control, and drip irrigation that would allow them to meet the supermarkets' specifications. With few people to buy their beans and tomatoes, the small farmers go into debt, lose their land, and end up in the *barrios* of the big cities or joining the stream of illegal immigrants to the United States.

Since structural adjustment policies were implemented in the mid-1980s, the economic growth rates of most debtor countries have declined significantly, along with their standard of living. Many of these countries are trapped in a vicious cycle: Low investment leads to greater unemployment, but there is no safety net for the unemployed because social spending is slashed, so then there is reduced consumption, which leads to low output, which causes low investment, and so it goes round and round. Ironically, some of the countries that are the most well integrated into the global economy are the ones that are the worst off. In poverty-stricken sub-Saharan Africa, for instance, exports account for 30 percent of the gross domestic product, compared to less than 20 percent for countries like England and the United States.

And here's the final outrage: The South has already paid its debt *several times over.* According to some estimates, between 1982 and 1998 indebted countries paid four times their original debts, while in that same period, because of exorbitant interest rates, their debt quadrupled. And 33 of the 41 most highly indebted Southern countries paid out three times as much in debt repayments annually as they received in aid from Northern governments and international aid agencies combined (Ehrenreich and Hochschild 2002, 267). Today, Southern countries are paying the North $717 million a day to service their debt—$12 billion a year from Africa alone. As long ago as 1991 a former director of the World Bank observed, "Not since the conquistadors plundered Latin America has the world experienced a flow in the direction we see today"—to which Jaggar adds: "The world has never experienced anything like the current flow" (Jaggar 2002, 121).

8.2. Neoliberalism

Most critics of the Southern debt believe that the theory of neoliberalism, which supposedly justifies IMF, WTO, and World Bank policies, is fatally flawed. (This is an instance of Lindemann's ad hoc rule Number 29: Behind almost everything that's wrong with the world, you'll find a batch of bad theory.) As Jaggar explains, neoliberalism represents a move away from the liberal social democracy of the post–Second World War era back to the laissez-faire liberalism of the Enlightenment, which held that the primary purpose of government was to allow the market to operate freely. *Neo*liberalism might therefore more aptly be named *retro*liberalism. Jaggar identifies four main doctrines of contemporary neoliberalism:

1. **"Free" trade.** Neoliberalism favors the elimination of import and export quotas and tariffs to promote the free flow of market goods. But it doesn't promote the free flow of labor. In fact, it actively seeks to control

that flow. Neoliberals' support of harsh border controls permits Northern businesses to move their factories to Southern countries with few occupational safety requirements, limited environmental restrictions, and very low wages. Neoliberalism's selective interpretation of 'free trade' also keeps immigrants from pursuing better jobs in Northern workplaces.

2. **Opposition to government regulation.** Neoliberalism opposes government regulation of wages, environmental protections, and working conditions on the grounds that such regulation presents an unfair barrier to free trade. Following this line of reasoning, poor working conditions, weak environmental regulations, and sweatshop wages give Southern countries a "competitive advantage"—but for whom?
3. **Refusal of responsibility for social welfare.** Neoliberalism presses governments to stop funding such things as housing, education, health care, old-age pensions, unemployment insurance, and services for people with disabilities, as these supposedly represent unfair subsidies to industry. The very few government expenditures judged *not* to be subsidies are those for defense and security, yet these underwrite a highly lucrative arms industry, not to mention private subcontractors who reap large profits by supplying goods and services to the military.
4. **Resource privatization.** Finally, neoliberalism favors private ownership of all economically exploitable resources, including public transportation, hydroelectric and nuclear power, health care, land, water, minerals, forests, and intellectual property. Rather than being regulated or some portion reserved for the common good, these resources are to be turned into profit-making enterprises and opened up for commercial exploitation in the global market.

Some of neoliberalism's flaws are already visible in this list, but they are magnified when we take gender into consideration. As Jaggar rightly points out, neoliberal globalization has made the lives of some women much better. But it has made the lives of the poor and the marginalized much worse, and as a disproportionate number of women are poor and marginalized, she concludes that neoliberal globalization is particularly bad for women. Here's why:

Problems with "free" trade. Women in the North—especially women of color—are often on the losing end of neoliberalism's selective understanding of free trade. When their previously well-paying jobs are moved from the North to low-wage areas in the South, these women are forced into part-time or poorly paid work, often in the service economy, which typically offers no health or retirement benefits. The livelihoods of many Southern women have also been lost because of free trade. In 2001 the United Nations reported, "Small women-run businesses often can't compete with cheap imported products brought in by trade liberalization. In Africa, many of women's traditional industries such as food processing and basket making are being wiped out. New employment opportunities have been created in some parts of Asia, but often with low wages and poor working conditions" (quoted in Jaggar 2002, 123). And as we'll see shortly, the jobs that Southern girls and women are forced into by neoliberal policies can expose them to positively horrifying abuse.

Problems with opposition to regulation. Women in particular are disadvantaged by the WTO's rejection of the Precautionary Principle, which tells countries to ban imported foods and drugs unless the manufacturers of these products can prove that they are safe. In other words, according to the Precautionary Principle, the burden of proof is on the manufacturers. Putting the burden of proof on *countries* to show that products are *not* safe, as the WTO does, poses a threat to children in particular, as they are especially likely to become ill from unsafe foods and drugs. And because the gendered division of labor assigns a vastly disproportionate amount of the care of children to women, it's women who must suffer the anxiety and distress of nursing the children harmed by the WTO's policy. The WTO's disregard for environmental protection laws also lays special burdens on women. In many Southern countries, the gendered division of labor assigns women the job of fetching water and firewood for her family. But in the absence of reforestation programs and clean water regulation, water pollution has become a general problem and firewood is often hard to find. So rural women are forced to walk farther and farther—sometimes as much as fifteen miles—in search of these necessities.

Problems with refusal of responsibility for social welfare. Because caring for children and ailing family members is women's work the world over, cutbacks in social programs are even harder on women than on men. In the North, mothers of young children forced by "Workfare" programs to work outside the home even if their wages can't buy adequate child care are still held responsible for their children's health and safety. In one particularly appalling instance, a mother with no other options left her two young children with her boyfriend on the first day of her job at McDonald's and returned home to find her three-year-old son in a coma. The little boy, who died in the hospital several hours later, had been severely beaten by the boyfriend for wetting his pants. The Tennessee court that heard the case, however, sentenced the *mother* to life in prison for "failure to protect" (Roberts 1999, 39).

In the global South, the widespread belief that a man will be cured of AIDS if he has sex with a virgin girl has proven difficult to combat, and cuts in public health services have only contributed to the problem. Reduction in health services has also contributed to a rise in the number of women dying in childbirth. And while the introduction of school fees in many Southern countries has put education out of reach for many poor families, those who can afford to educate only some of their children are most likely to send the boys to school and put the girls to work at home.

Problems with resource privatization. Putting public lands, water, forests, and health care into private ownership also hurts women in particular. Multinational corporations have patented seeds, including indigenous seeds, and can therefore charge high prices for them. In many parts of the global South, where the gendered division of labor assigns the work of farming to women, it's women who must pay those prices and women who must find other sources of income when they can't afford to farm any more.

In the global North, the WTO's defense of intellectual property rights has supported the pharmaceutical industry's practice of patenting drugs, which keeps prices high by eliminating any competition. This is a problem for the poor particularly in the United States, where, as we've seen, there is no centralized system of health care financing that controls the market and sets limits on spending. Drug companies justify their patents on the grounds that the profits they generate are used to finance research on new medicines, but that's not where most of the money goes. According to its annual report for 2003, for example, the drug manufacturer Merck spent 28 percent of its revenues on "marketing and administration," kept 30 percent as profit, and invested only 14 percent in research and development—much of it, if the industry's track record on the whole is any guide, on copycat drugs that have only a slightly different formula from drugs already on the market. The high cost of pharmaceuticals in the United States hurts women more than men because elderly people are the largest consumers of drugs, and elderly women, who reach retirement with smaller pensions and other assets than men do, outnumber elderly men by ten to seven.

8.3. The Global Version of Women's Work

The neoliberal form of globalism, then, doesn't stand up very well to feminist ethical analysis. Matters only get worse when you take a close look at how the work that gender assigns to women has itself been globalized. It's globalized not only in the sense that policies of "debt" repayment and the inability to compete in global markets have taken women's traditional livelihoods away from them, but also in the sense that women must migrate from the global South to the global North to find work that is open to them. Some go from Southeast Asia to the oil-rich Middle East, Hong Kong, Malaysia, and Singapore. Others go from the former USSR to western Europe. Still others migrate from south to north in the Americas, and a fourth route takes women from Africa to France and Italy. I'm going to concentrate on the three kinds of work that most typically takes these women so far from their homes and families: domestic work, nursing, and sex work.

Domestic Work

Feminist theorists such as Heidi Hartmann and Joan Tronto find domestic work, which encompasses both child care and housework, inherently exploitative. Hartmann claims that housework puts men in control of women's labor power and is therefore an oppressive "mode of production," while Tronto argues that the practice of hiring nannies to accomplish the child care work of upper-middle-class households is unjust and furthers social inequality. While Tronto and Hartmann are surely right in condemning the abusive power systems of class and gender that force women into work that the powerful don't want to do, it's a mistake, I think, to devalue the work itself as undesirable and not worth doing. In fact, to turn up one's nose at domestic work is to dismiss it precisely the way gender does: It's only women's work, so it goes unacknowledged and unappreciated.

Housework isn't to everyone's liking, but many people, myself included, enjoy polishing and scrubbing. A good deal of pleasure can be derived from a simmering soup-pot and the smell of fresh-baked bread, and the care of a two-year-old can be at least as fascinating as it is exasperating. Compare the intrinsic interest, variety, and satisfaction of jobs like these to assembly-line work and there's no contest. When women who do domestic work are paid well and treated with respect, they are arguably at least as well off as anyone else who works for wages. In the global economy, however, even when the pay is good the work can be bad, and too often it can be very bad indeed.

Because of the growing economic gap between the global North and the global South, the middle class of Southern countries now earns less than the poor of the North. For instance, women who in their native Philippines averaged $176 a month as middle-class teachers, clerical workers, and nurses can earn $700 a month in Italy or $1,400 a month in Los Angeles by working as lower-class nannies, maids, and care-service workers (Ehrenreich and Hochschild 2002, 18). And because more middle-class women in the North work outside the home than they once did, there is a greater demand for domestic workers in Northern countries. Southern women supply that demand.

The fact that they have *migrated* to do this work, however, puts them at a disadvantage in a number of respects, while the fact that the work is *domestic* puts them at a further disadvantage. For starters, many if not most women migrants have young children of their own who can't come with them, and while it's to support these children that the women have migrated in the first place, the separation from their children burdens them with what is sometimes overwhelming sorrow. It's hard on the children, too: They are more frequently ill, express more anger and confusion, do considerably less well in school, and are more likely to commit suicide than children whose mothers have not gone abroad (Ehrenreich and Hochschild 2002, 22).

Second, because many migrant workers are undocumented and terrified of deportation, they initially look on the privacy of the house where they work as a boon because it shields them from the police. But privacy cuts both ways: It also shields employers from public view and public censure, so they can treat their servants pretty much any way they like. What employers demand can be simply degrading. The researcher and activist Bridget Anderson offers the following examples: "cleaning cats' anuses, flushing employers' toilets, scrubbing the floor with a toothbrush three times a day, or standing by the door in the same position for hours at a time" (quoted in Ehrenreich and Hochschild 2002, 107–108). Even when the employer treats the maid or nanny as one of the family, however, there is potential for abuse: being "one of the family" often serves as an excuse for longer working hours, erratic pay, lack of privacy, and no time off (Romero 1997, 157–59).

In the worst cases, migrant domestic workers are enslaved. Ruth Gnizako, for example, was promised a house and a car if she would leave West Africa and come to suburban Maryland to work as a housekeeper and nanny for the five children of a World Bank employee and his wife. When she arrived she found that there was no house or car. Instead, she was required to sleep with a pair of one-year-old twins in her arms every night, and when the family went out, she had to wait outside the apartment in the hallway until they returned. The couple repeatedly beat her, but when the police arrived after the neighbors called in response to her screams, they couldn't understand her broken French. This gave the banker the opportunity to suggest that Gnizako was crazy, so the police took her to a mental health facility, where she was forcibly sedated and her arms and legs tied to the bedposts. By the time the doctors found an interpreter, Gnizako was so incoherent from the sedation that she couldn't explain what had been done to her. She was returned to the family, where she endured many more months of beatings and exhausting work before the neighbors were able to free her and get help. She eventually went back to West Africa, but without managing to collect a penny of the wages the banker and his wife owed her (Ehrenreich and Hochschild 2002, 143–44).

The scholar and activist Joy Zarembka traces a *pattern* of abuse for immigrants who come to the United States to do domestic work. Typically, she says, the woman's employer illegally takes away her passport and other travel documents, and if there was a signed contract, that too is confiscated and replaced with one stipulating longer hours and lower pay—in some cases, no pay at all. The domestic worker is forbidden to leave the house by herself, use the phone, make friends, or even talk to people. She's often denied health insurance and Social Security. She might be given as a gift to her employer's mistress or loaned to another family. She could be required to sleep on the floor, sometimes in the kitchen, unfurnished basement, or laundry room. One woman was forced to wear a dog collar and occasionally had to sleep outside with the family's dogs (Ehrenreich and Hochschild 2002, 142–54).

If the domestic worker complains, her employer can threaten to send her home or turn her over to the police. And indeed, U.S. immigration law is against her: When a woman flees an abusive employer she goes "out of status," which makes her ineligible for other jobs in the United States and puts her at risk of being deported. Not all employers rely on the law, though, since psychological coercion can work just as well as the legal kind. A dark-skinned Brazilian named Hilda Rosa Dos Santos, for example, lived for twenty years as a prisoner-housekeeper with no pay and little food, after her employers convinced her that Americans hated black people so much that she'd be raped or killed if she ever went outside. Similarly, an Indonesian maid was told that it was unsafe to go out because Americans are so hostile to Muslims (Ehrenreich and Hochschild 2002, 146–47).

Unable to speak much of the language of their host country, cut off from their culture and from the support that co-workers would offer, unaware of their rights under the law, and not knowing where to go for help, domestic workers are silent, invisible laborers in the global economy. That so many continue to migrate to the North speaks volumes for their courage, hope, and desperation, but reflects as well the destructive social forces that have shaped the world in which they must live.

Nursing

Like domestic work, nursing can be quite satisfying and rewarding, and it's just as much a mistake to think that there is something inherently degrading about it as it is to be contemptuous of the work of nannies or maids. Whether nursing is in fact satisfying depends, again like domestic work, on the conditions under which it is practiced. Because nursing is highly gendered—the International Council on Nursing says that 95 percent of nurses, worldwide, are women—and because nursing takes place within a medical hierarchy with doctors on the top and nurses on the bottom, it participates in two power systems, one of which is certainly oppressive and the other apt to be so.

There is no doubt that the work can be dangerous. To cite (again) statistics issued by the International Council on Nursing:

- Health care workers are more likely to be attacked at work than prison guards or police officers.
- Nurses are the health care workers most at risk, with female nurses considered the most vulnerable.
- General patient rooms have replaced psychiatric units at the second most frequent area for assaults.
- Physical assault is almost exclusively perpetrated by patients.
- Seventy-two percent of nurses don't feel safe from assault in their workplace.
- Up to 95 percent of nurses reported having been bullied at work.
- Up to 75 percent of nurses reported having been subjected to sexual harassment at work.

Because nursing is skilled work requiring considerable education, nurses can find jobs in even the most impoverished

Southern countries. But because countries in the North pay much better, many Southern nurses migrate to Northern countries, which creates a nursing shortage at home. And because nursing education is often heavily subsidized by Southern governments, these countries lose not only well-trained and valuable workers, but also their returns on an expensive investment.

In the United States, where 92 percent of nurses are women, more than 23,000 foreigners took the nurse licensing exam in 2003. Of these, more than half were from the Philippines. Beginning in 1982, the Filipino government encouraged girls to train as nurses, deliberately engineering a surplus so that nurses would migrate to Northern countries and send back foreign currency in the form of remittances to their families. This strategy was so successful, according to a 17 May 2003 article in the *Manila Times,* that nearly 34,000 nurses went abroad between 1995 and 2000, and currently between 40 and 60 percent leave every year for jobs overseas. It's not hard to see why: In the Philippines, nurses in urban areas earn only $150 a month, whereas in the United States the average salary is more than $3,000 a month.

There are two catches, though. The first is that the Philippines is now experiencing a serious nursing shortage, with no end in sight. The problem is compounded by internal migration: Because nurses in the rural communities migrate to urban areas and high-tech hospitals to get the experience they need to be hired overseas, health care in rural and remote areas, which is already inadequate, has become even more patchy. The second catch is that, like Filipina domestic workers, many of the nurses have to leave their young children behind when they emigrate, and even though they send home money and try to stay in touch by phone, the separation is typically very painful for them and their children.

The UK has imported its own share of overseas-trained nurses—almost 13,000 in 2003 alone. While 43 percent of these are Filipinas, nurses from India are fast catching up as the second-largest group of nurses from abroad. At about 6,000 rupees a month, or $120, Indian nurses make even less money than Filipina nurses do, but what lures them to the North isn't just money, it's lack of appreciation at home.

The Indian Health Minister, Anbumani Ramadoss, recently acknowledged that nurses were "a neglected lot" and that the general public didn't recognize their work while physicians often took credit for it. At the same time, though, he said he often received complaints about nurses' behaving impatiently toward their patients. "Your logo and motto," he told the Student Nurses Association, "should be smile and serve."

Jamaica likewise loses nurses to the U.S. and the UK, at the rate of 8 percent of its RNs and 20 percent of its specialist nurses annually. The country is so poor that it can ill afford to lose any of its skilled workers; the exodus abroad threatens the health of the population along with the well-being of the children who are left behind. Jamaica has only 11 nurses for every 10,000 people, compared to 97 nurses per 10,000 people in the United States, yet the U.S. actively recruits nurses from its Southern neighbor.

The North has siphoned off a frightening number of nurses from Africa. Over the last fifteen years, Ghana has lost close to 60 percent of its nurses, even though the country trains about 600 new ones every year. In some hospitals, wards built for 40 patients, which should have 6 or 7 nurses on duty at night, are staffed by only one nurse and a non-professional nurse's aid. Mauritius too has highly advanced nurse-training programs, but like Ghana it can't compete with European countries that pay ten times what nurses make at home. So, despite its investments in education, the Northern migration leaves Mauritian hospitals understaffed. According to a 28 May 2004 article in *afrol News,* global migration has left the public maternity hospital in Nairobi, Kenya, so short of nurses that a single professional often cares for 60 to 90 patients on shifts that last ten hours. One exhausted nurse who chose not to emigrate said, "Yes, we are basically volunteers. But if we didn't stay, then who would take care of these mothers and babies? . . . The nurses here are paid very low salaries, very low. You get just 5,000 shillings a month [$70], but you cannot survive on that amount!" South Africa's relative prosperity makes it a slightly more attractive place in which to practice nursing than many other African countries, but since 1991 the number of nurses leaving the country has risen eightfold: Three hundred trained nurses now leave South Africa every *month.* This leaves the nurses who remain with ridiculously heavy workloads, and it seriously compromises patient care. For all of Africa, the effects of globalization on nursing are all the more devastating because of the epidemic of HIV/AIDS that is ravaging the continent.

Sex Work

According to a number of feminist sex workers themselves, sex work is no more inherently degrading than other forms of work—and it can pay much better. To look down on it, they argue, is to value it the way gender does, by drawing a connection between bodies (especially women's bodies) and impurity, categorizing women as either madonnas or whores, and regarding sex itself as basically shameful. Other feminists are divided on the issue of whether sex work, considered apart from the conditions under which it's practiced, is demeaning and beneath human dignity. What's generally agreed on, though, is that even under optimal conditions, sex work is often exploitative, especially in countries (like the U.S.) where prostitution is generally illegal. Under conditions of globalization, this exploitation increases by several orders of magnitude.

The international sex trade has become a major industry, converting millions of women and children into sexual commodities that generate billions of dollars' worth of profits for their investors. The rapid growth in prostitution and allied enterprises—massage parlors, lap-dancing clubs, pornography, and so on—depends on a black-market economy run by pimps who are connected to organized crime. Greatly benefiting from this economy are the international hotel chains, tourist bureaus, and airlines that make large-scale sex tourism possible. Consumers from the global North can now hop on a plane and have access to young—very young—girls' bodies in Brazil, Cuba, Kenya, the Philippines, Nicaragua, Russia, Sri Lanka, Thailand, and Vietnam. Or they can stay at home in Amsterdam, Berlin, Chicago, London, New York, Paris, and other major cities where underage imports from the global South are available for their pleasure. The CIA estimates that between 18,000 and 20,000 sex workers are trafficked annually into the United States alone.

Many girls go into sex work willingly, given their limited options, in the hope that their clients will be possible tickets out of poverty. Chinese girls flock to brothels in Japan and Thailand, returning home to recruit their sisters and friends. Girls from Eastern Europe and the former Soviet Union service sex tourists in Hamburg's Reeperbahn, Berlin's Kurfürstendamm, Paris's Montmartre, and the red-light districts of Amsterdam and Rotterdam, where prostitution is not only legal but has become an important tourist draw as well. In the Dominican Republic, a popular vacation spot for German sex tourists, freelance sex workers look to their clients as potential providers of money, marriage, and visas, though only a few manage to leave the island—and poverty—behind.

Increasingly, however, women and children have become new raw resources lured to industrialized areas through false promises and held captive by physical and economic force. In Thailand, for example, although prostitution is illegal, the country's industrialization and its social acceptance of prostitution have contributed to a flourishing system of sex slavery. The sociologist Kevin Bales estimates that of roughly a million prostitutes in Thailand, some 35,000 are now slaves—many more than ever before in the country's history. When the area around Bangkok, in the middle of Thailand, became industrialized in the 1980s and 90s, the mountainous, northern part of the country was left in poverty. Prices increased as the economy grew, and the demand for refrigerators, TVs, cars, and other consumer goods increased as well. Succumbing to temptation, many families in the north who traditionally might have sold a daughter to redeem a mortgaged farm now sell her to finance a luxury item. According to a recent survey of the mountain provinces, two-thirds of families who sold their daughters could afford to keep them but "preferred to buy color televisions and video equipment" instead (Ehrenreich and Hochschild 2002, 211).

Typically, a Thai woman who herself comes from a northern village acts as a broker, approaching village families with promises of well-paid work for their daughters. The parents, understanding that the work is probably prostitution but having only the vaguest idea of what that involves, negotiate with the broker and are paid around 50,000 baht (roughly $2,000)—easily a year's income for families living in rural poverty. The girl, usually between 12 and 16 years of age, is then taken south by the broker, where she is sold for 100,000 baht to the brothel where she will work. If she tries to run away she is raped and beaten to make her submissive, but what really holds her in bondage is debt. She might be told that she owes the brothel 200,000 baht, that the rent she must pay for her room is an additional 30,000 baht per month, that she'll be charged for food, drink, and doctor's fees, and that she'll be fined if she doesn't please her customers. On average, 15 men will buy her each night, paying 200 baht ($7.50) apiece. About half of that 200 is supposed to be credited against the girl's debt, rent, and other expenses, another 200 goes to her pimp, and 100 goes to the brothel. Never mind that the figures don't add up—that's how the debt grows, keeping the girl under complete control as long as she's of any value to the brothel owner and the pimp.

It's in the brothel owner's interest to let the girl send a little money home regularly after a year or so, as the high demand for young HIV-negative girls makes it useful for owners to cultivate village families to ensure a steady supply of daughters. AIDS is a serious problem, however; if the monthly HIV test turns positive, the girl will be thrown out to starve. In any case, Bales notes, the working life of a Thai sex slave is no more than about two to five years. After that, "It's more cost-effective to discard her and replace her with someone fresh" (Ehrenreich and Hochschild 2002, 220).

Sex slavery isn't confined to Thailand. The Japanese mob maintains brothels and bars that traffic in slaves whom they control with extreme violence: Because the girls typically enter the country under false passports, mob members seldom hesitate to kill them once they stop being profitable or have angered their owners. Mexican associations of pimps operate as wholesalers, collecting female "merchandise" and taking orders from brothels in the major U.S. sex-trafficking hubs of New York, Los Angeles, Atlanta, and Chicago. In Moscow, Kiev, and other East European cities where poverty has soared since the collapse of the Soviet Union, sex-trafficking rings lure girls with the promise of modeling, acting, and child care jobs in Western Europe and the United States.

Some of these girls suspect that prostitution might be involved, but as Donna Hughes, a specialist in sex trafficking, puts it, "Their idea of prostitution is *Pretty Woman,* which is one of the most popular films in Ukraine and Russia. They're thinking, This may not be so bad." But it is so bad. Working at the rate of 20 men per day, these girls bring in as much as $30,000 a week, though they see none of this money and the sex is usually rough. Typically, sex slaves in the United States, like those in Thailand, last only two to five years. After that they may be killed in the brothel or dumped and deported. But they can't go home. As one of them lament, "We're way too damaged to give back. A lot of these children never wanted to see their parents again after a while, because what do you tell your parents? What are you going to say? You're no good" (*New York Times Magazine,* 25 January 2004, pp. 36, 75).

When you combine a careful *description* of how gender operates in the current system of globalization with normative judgments that *criticize* and *correct* both the theory and the practice of globalization, the resulting picture is not a pretty one. It shows us a power system that disguises its oppression of Southern countries by calling it debt, and it invokes neoliberalism—a theory rigged in its own favor—to justify its policies. The consequences for women in both the South and the North are, as we have seen, often burdensome and sometimes horrendous.

8.4. Cross-Cultural Judgments

Globalization also raises a different set of worries. In an era of intense and extensive international trade and travel, people are aware to a greater extent than ever before of the differences between other cultures and their own. Some of these differences—say, the practice of female genital cutting in parts of Africa or dowry murders in India—have been subjected to harsh criticism not only by Northern feminists but by U.S. and European governments as well. And that sort of criticism is the worry here. When it's a Northern culture judging a Southern one, are cross-cultural judgments a form of cultural imperialism?

You'll recall, from Chapter Two, that Iris Marion Young identifies cultural imperialism as one of the five faces of oppression: "Cultural imperialism involves the universalization of a dominant group's experience and culture, and its establishment as the norm" (Young 1990, 59). It's the unjustified use of the dominant group's standards to judge other groups, and it happens because the dominant group takes its own experiences, achievements, and values to be representative of all people, everywhere. So when, for example, people in the United States condemn *sati*—the practice in India of widows' burning themselves to death on their husband's funeral pyres—aren't these Americans just imposing their own values on an ancient and venerable culture with different values of its own?

For feminists, the worry is a real one, since they are acutely aware of the hardship and injustice that comes from not respecting differences among people. But at the same time, it seems wrong to stand by and do nothing when systemic abuse of a social group—especially of women—goes on in any part of the world. Take, for instance, the practice of clitoridectomy, about which Nahid Toubia, a Sudanese surgeon and expert on female genital cutting, writes: "The male equivalent of clitoridectomy (in which all or part of the clitoris is removed) would be the amputation of most of the penis. The male equivalent of infibulation (which involves not only clitoridectomy, but the removal of or closing off of most of the sensitive tissues around the vagina) would be the removal of all of the penis, its roots of soft tissue, and part of the scrotal skin" (quoted in Okin 1998, 49). The political theorist Susan Moller Okin reports that in 1996, when the spokesman for the U.S. Embassy to the Ivory Coast was asked about clitoridectomy, he said, "It's a matter for local society to determine the extent to which these practices are to be tolerated." As cavalier as that sounds, he was outdone by the Ivory Coast's French embassy spokesman, who said, "This is a marginal problem." Then, perhaps as an afterthought, he added, "It's important, but to feed people is probably more important" (quoted in Okin 1998, 37).

We should be outraged by this kind of moral callousness, shouldn't we? If we don't speak up, aren't we just abandoning these women to their fate? But then, if we *do* speak up, aren't we just imposing our Northern ideas of liberty, equality, and rights on non-Northern cultures?

The feminist philosopher Uma Narayan diagnoses the problem of cross-cultural judgments differently. She thinks the problem isn't one of having to choose between callousness and imperialism, but of avoiding what she calls *cultural essentialism.* Too often, she believes, the well-intentioned desire to respect differences among people results in the use of totalizing categories that replicate colonialist and racist assumptions: "Western culture," "Southern women," "Indian culture," "African women," are treated as if each group is different from the others but within each group everyone is alike. This, she argues, is to reproduce the sharply contrasting essentialist picture of "Western culture" versus "Others" that colonial governments used to justify their rule—as, for instance, when they argued that it was the "white man's burden" to bring Western civilization to "the natives." Ironically, various nationalist movements have used this same sharp contrast to challenge and overthrow colonial rule; their appeals to "national culture and traditions" as ancient, unchanging, and sanctioned by religious texts gave an identity to fledgling nations that distinguished them from the cultures of their colonial oppressors.

The essentialist contrast drawn by a number of Northern feminists between "Western culture" and "Others," says the feminist theorist Chandra Mohanty, produces this picture:

> The average third world [Southern] woman leads an essentially truncated life based on her feminine gender (read: sexually constrained) and her being "third world" (read: ignorant, poor, uneducated, tradition-bound, domestic, family-oriented, victimized, etc.). This, I suggest, is in contrast to the (implicit) self-representation of Western women as educated, as modern, as having control over their own bodies and sexualities, and the freedom to make their own decisions. (Quoted in Narayan 1998, 91)

At the same time, because nationalization movements are equally prone to essentializing their cultures (though in very different terms), they often pressure women to conform to culturally dominant norms of femininity as a way of "preserving national culture," and condemn as cultural traitors those feminists who challenge practices within Southern countries that demean women.

One way to resist cultural essentialism, says Narayan, is to stop assuming that cultures are natural givens, static and unchanging, and start thinking of them as human constructs with specific histories that are deployed for a number of political ends. Narayan explains, for example, that *sati* (widow burning) was not considered particularly representative of Indian culture until colonial times, when the British became deeply fascinated by it. She speculates that what both attracted and repelled them about the practice was that wifely self-sacrifice was a value with which they were deeply familiar, yet burning oneself to death as a funeral offering was deeply alien to them. The British could therefore applaud the "nobility" of widows who engaged in the practice while simultaneously feeling disgust at the "savagery" of self-immolation. In short, to categorize *sati* as a central Indian tradition despite the fact that the vast majority even of Hindu communities never practiced it, let alone Indian ones, allowed the British to define themselves as enlightened in contrast to the brown-skinned Other (Narayan 1997, 61–66). Narayan argues that *sati*'s status as an Indian cultural tradition was an *effect* of the prolonged debate over its centrality to Indian culture. "As a result of this debate," she observes, "*sati* came to acquire, for both British and Indians, and for its supporters as well as its opponents, an 'emblematic status,' becoming a larger-than-life symbol of 'Hindu' and 'Indian' culture in a way that transcended the actual facts of its limited practice" (Narayan 1997, 65).

Narayan is careful to point out that it's not only colonizers such as the British, Dutch, or Spanish who appealed to cultural traditions for their own political purposes. The dominant members of once-colonized cultures also invoke "culture-defining practices" when it suits them—particularly if a proposed cultural change poses a threat to the dominant group's social power. In Sierra Leone, for example, almost none of the elaborate rituals and training that used to take place in the year or two before a girl's genital excision are still observed, largely because the time, money, and social infrastructure that supported these rituals are no longer available. However, the excision itself, practiced apart from the context in which it used to be embedded, is still seen as crucial to preserving cultural tradition. The disappearance of the rituals and training that used to be the main point of the coming-of-age ceremony seems to have modified the practice for the worse, in that the age at which excision is carried out has drastically decreased. Whereas it used to be done to teenagers who were old enough to learn the ceremonies and undergo the initiation, excision is now performed on little girls, some as young as three or four years old, who can't understand what's being done to them (Narayan 1998, 94–95).

When feminists protest practices of this sort, they are sometimes told that equality and rights are Northern values whose extension to the South is "imperialist." Arguably, though, it's as a result of the political struggles by excluded and marginalized groups in both the global North *and* South that doctrines of equality and rights slowly came to be seen as applicable to the South as well. One way to think of what's at work here is to return to the discussion in Chapter Five of an ethics of responsibility. That ethics, recall, bids us to think of morality as something we do together, and it "both presupposes and seeks a continuing common life" (Walker 1998, 63). What people do morally together is limited by, but also made mutually intelligible by, a background of shared beliefs about what's right and good, what people are supposed to do, and what people can expect from one another—what Margaret Urban Walker calls moral understandings. Moral understandings are not limited to individual cultures but often cross national boundaries, particularly among groups of people who are committed to the same values. Because feminists all over the world are committed to the idea that oppressing women is wrong and that women's experiences deserve to be taken seriously, they share a powerful set of moral understandings that can cross the North–South divide.

Resisting cultural essentialism—including the cultural relativism that serves the purposes of dominant members of a culture—doesn't entail a simpleminded opposition to generalizations of every kind. Consider these two statements:

1. "Prostitution is still the main if not the only source of work for African women."
2. "Women continue to be discriminated against all over the world and are subject to many forms of violence."

The first generalization is not only empirically false but disrespectful to Africans, because it contemptuously rolls many quite different cultures into one essence labeled "African," and then makes a nonsensical claim about them. The second generalization, I'd argue, is true and politically useful, because it draws attention to harms done to women in many national contexts, while leaving room for attention to differences in the kinds of discrimination and forms of violence that particular groups of women suffer.

Let's by all means object to what the professor of Afro-American studies Kwame Anthony Appiah calls "Eurocentric hegemony posing as universalism" (Narayan 1998, 104). But let's object, as well, to cultural homogeneity posing as "respect for difference." True respect for ways of life other than your own requires that you drop the idea that yours is the first and only culture, and that you drop as well the reproduction of obnoxious cultural stereotypes. Then, when you know the *complexity* of a culture other than your own, and you know its *history,* and you know how *widespread* a particular practice is and the different *forms* it can take, and you've considered *analogs* to the practice within your own culture, and you know what *feminists in that culture* think of the practice, you are in a position to make judgments that genuinely respect cultural difference. It's through something like this amount of effort that we can, in the end, create a global feminism.

These close-ups of feminist approaches to bioethics, violence, and globalization are little more than line drawings, capturing a general impression but leaving out many of the details. Equally sketchy are the overviews of feminism, feminist concepts, identity theory, dominant moral theories, and feminist moral theories that preceded them. You've been given only one or two glimpses of the rich array of thoughts and ideas that become possible when the fact of gender is taken seriously as a subject for scholarly study. This book is your invitation to get further acquainted with what's going on in feminist ethics. I hope you'll want to come in. The door is open.

For Further Reading

Ehrenreich, Barbara, and Arlie Russell Hochschild, eds. 2002. *Global Woman: Nannies, Maids, and Sex Workers in the New Economy.* New York: Henry Holt Owl.

Jaggar, Alison M. 2002. "A Feminist Critique of the Alleged Southern Debt." *Hypatia* 17 (4): 199–42.

Narayan, Uma. 1997. *Dislocating Cultures: Identities, Traditions, and Third World Feminism.* New York: Routledge.

———. 1998. "Essence of Culture and a Sense of History: A Feminist Critique of Cultural Essentialism." *Hypatia* 13 (2): 86–106.

Okin, Susan Moller. 1998. "Feminism, Women's Human Rights, and Cultural Differences." *Hypatia* 13 (2): 32–52.

Roberts, Dorothy E. 1999. "Mothers Who Fail to Protect Their Children: Accounting for Private and Public Responsibility." Pp. 31–49 in *Mother Troubles: Rethinking Contemporary Maternal Dilemmas.* Ed. Julia E. Hanigsberg and Sara Ruddick. Boston: Beacon.

Romero, Mary. 1997. "Who Takes Care of the Maid's Children? Exploring the Costs of Domestic Service." Pp. 151–69 in *Feminism and Families.* Ed. Hilde Lindemann Nelson. New York: Routledge.

Walker, Margaret Urban. 1998. *Moral Understandings: A Feminist Study in Ethics.* New York: Routledge.

Young, Iris Marion. 1990. *Justice and the Politics of Difference.* Princeton: Princeton University Press.

Index